CHASING THE LOST CITY
Chronicles of Discovery in Honduras

by
Tom Weinberg

D1216022

COPYRIGHT

First edition published by Eckhartz Press

ISBN: 978-0-9985171-0-0

Copyright © Tom Weinberg 2017

Designed by Elan Soltes

www.chasingthelostcity.com

Printed by Unwork, Inc.
813 SE 10th Avenue
Portland, OR 97214

TABLE OF CONTENTS

PART ONE: MY STORY

February 2015—I was 70 years old, a desk-sitting urban Jewish TV/video guy who had never spent a night sleeping on the ground in a jungle. I hadn't camped out at all for decades.

I've always had a roof over my head—and a wet tent in sloppy rain forest mud doesn't qualify. I detested Boy Scouts and was an early dropout. And I couldn't hear much either, unless the sounds were coming from right in front of my face. Thankfully, I had state-of-the-art hearing aids in my ears that worked all the time I was in the jungle.

So, you can see I wasn't likely to be the MVP Explorer in the **Mosquitia Jungle** of Honduras, one of the wildest and most dense spots anywhere in the Americas.

But, I knew I had to go. I had to see for myself if what we thought was there really existed. Was there a Lost City? Were we really going to find it deep in the jungle?

As you probably know by now, there was and we did.

It began for me in 1994, when my friend since the 70s, **Steve Elkins**, and I first got in cahoots to track down the Lost City. He had been in Honduras in 1994 on a video shoot searching for a place known as **Ciudad Blanca**, the **White City**, also called **The Lost City of the Monkey God**. It had been a legend for centuries. Stories of Ciudad Blanca were written about in the 1500s by Spanish Conquistadors. Indigenous people knew about it for centuries before that.

•

In the 20th century, many adventurers claimed to have found evidence of a civilization, although nobody had photographic proof or a map of the place. But we were hell bent to be the discoverers. Starting in 1994, we figured out the most likely location of the city, used scientific laser technology to uncover ancient structures on the jungle floor, then went there and made a movie, showing it in living color. What we found might not be THE Lost City of the Monkey God, or Ciudad Blanca, but there is incontrovertible evidence (actual relics) of an ancient people whose identity still remains unknown.

For Steve and me, the search became something of an obsession, gnawing at our lives for more than 20 years. It was an itch we scratched every way we could imagine. Finally, in February 2015, we (mostly Steve) had put together a group of about 20 archaeologists, video/filmmakers, mapping professionals, helicopter pilots, and jungle survival experts, and teamed with the Honduran government to enter and hang out in the isolated Mosquitia jungle of Northeastern Honduras.

It was and is the closest thing to the Garden of Eden that any of us has ever experienced.

On the day our group found dozens of unexplainable ancient artifacts on an earthen pyramid, Steve and I sat by his tent ruminating. He said: "No matter what happens from now on, I feel vindicated. We were right!"

We all feel the need to be right, but it's elevated for Elkins because he had spent thousands of waking hours (and, no doubt, some in his sleep) concentrating on the science, exploration, and logistics of getting in and out of that jungle and finding out what's there. It's almost in his DNA to theorize, learn, test, and prove. His wife Janet called the two of us "The Lost Boys" for many years. We didn't enjoy admitting it, but it was an accurate name. Neither she nor anyone else could believe that we never gave up.

Although we were both obsessed with finding the Lost City, I had a different monkey on my back: I wanted to discover it and show it to the world on TV. I've produced more than 500 nonfiction shows. None was as far-reaching or as impossible to do as this one.

Even so, it never occurred to me that it might have been a wild goose chase, or worse, a disaster.

We both felt a lifetime's worth of relief and accomplishment in that late afternoon conversation in February, 2015. A pair of spider monkeys seemed to be having a parallel conversation on a branch about 40 feet above us. We were in their space. They'd probably never seen apes like us and they let us know by screeching and dropping stuff on us. Within a week, our group had left their space, but that jungle will never be the same.

Nor will we.

I put my butt on the line for this project.

What You're Reading

I have assembled my writing about our discovery of a Lost City, now officially called "City of the Jaguar." I wrote two sets of chronicles during my stays in Honduras—one in 2012, the other in 2015. Nearly every night I wrote my personal impressions of our journeys into the unknown.

In 2012, we were using **LiDAR (Light Detection And Ranging)** laser techniques to see through the jungle canopy. That let us discover what was there on the ground. I wrote 17 chronicles on that trip. Then, in 2015, I wrote 12 chronicles during our ground-truthing jungle expedition. Those chronicles are the core of this book. Each is dated and is almost exactly as I wrote it on my laptop at the time. I approached it as a daily assignment, kind of like a beat reporter with a deadline. I have added pictures, but haven't changed the chronicles. They are more than half the pages of this book. The rest I wrote later in 2015 and in 2016, to express my feelings after more than 20 years of involvement. I am addicted to writing, so my primary motivation was my need to tell my personal story and for you to read it.

To find out the whole story, you must read **Douglas Preston's** terrific book, *The Lost City of the Monkey God*, published in January, 2017. It is comprehensive and brilliantly written, documenting the history, archaeology, medical implications, and thrills of the entire adventure. It's the big picture.

I've limited this book to my own experiences and the visual impressions of what was the adventure of my lifetime. The pictures are from several sources starting with **UTL Productions** (from frames in our video) and master photographer **Roberto Ysais**, who was with us in Roatan in 2012.

I'm A Where Guy

Perseverance is a main theme of the histories of explorers and seekers, whether in the Mosquitia Jungle or anywhere else. Of course, one person's perseverance is another's obsession, but I don't want to go there right now.

I just reread *Jungleland*, journalist **Christopher Stewart's** 2013 book about his exploration in the Mosquitia. His obsession was **Theodore Morde**—finding out and telling the most minute details of Morde's 1940 exploration. He was piggybacking on Morde's need to go into the unknown and find artifacts—stuff nobody had ever brought to the boss, the big rich **George Heye** in New York City.

With the latest research by Douglas Preston, we now know that Morde was a fraud. The artifacts he picked up—the ones that went into the Smithsonian—weren't from the heart of the jungle at all. He got them near the ocean in one afternoon. He was really looking for gold. In his private journals he wrote that he was absolutely convinced there was NO Lost City in the Mosquitia. Despite that, he took credit for discovering one and became a famous hero in 1940. Morde never went back to Honduras, despite his promises to do so, and he committed suicide fifteen years after his famous self-proclaimed "discovery."

Me, I just knew that Ciudad Blanca—or at least the place in a valley that we first tracked via satellite in 1996 and then with LiDAR in 2012—was a place nobody else had likely been for centuries.

That's what always turned me on. When I was 8 or 10, tromping through the ravines near my home in the Ravinia neighborhood of Highland Park, IL, I consciously thought about the place I was walking/standing and that it hadn't been stepped on since the times when the Indians (that's what we called them then) wandered through on their way to Lake Michigan.

I loved that idea—that I was somewhere special. It made me feel special, unlike any of the other kids who stayed on the sidewalk—and definitely not like the dads who went on the train five mornings a week to Chicago's Loop or the moms who, from what I could tell, were fully occupied with their in-the-house lives. For any of those adults, finding virgin patches of earth down in the ravines wasn't who they were or what they thought about. Maybe there was a time when they did, but they'd probably given up and buried it in adult life decades earlier.

In my teens, I spent five summers out West, mostly in the Colorado Rocky Mountains at Vagabond Ranch for boys and girls—a place the owners, the Paveks, didn't want to call "a camp." We rode horses, fished for trout in the creeks, did ranch work on fences, houses, barns and stables, and loaded into woody DeSoto station wagons to camp out, mostly in national parks. I loved seeing new places. I did all that, but what had the biggest impact was hiking to unnamed spots on hilltops and planting my booted or Conversed feet on untrampled places and having those same powerful "nobody has been in this exact spot" feelings.

I've tried to figure out why I spent all those years chasing after something that might not even exist. And in 2017 I got the answer—I had spent my first 50 years becoming aware of the uniqueness of where I was and what it took to be there.

For me, the driving force in the exploration wasn't so much the buried objects that might be in the jungle or the people who had been there, or even the legend of gold or monkey god effigies. Those were the cool material things, "the excuses" that everyone could understand as motivation, the same as dozens before us. For me the tingle, the drive, the thing that has always taken over whatever else I was doing, is the gut-need to go to and experience what it feels like to be in an unknown place on the earth, no matter how big or small.

We were all taught that Balboa "discovered" the Pacific Ocean—though non-European people had been there for centuries. Huh? He was driven to go to the next unknown place. That's the deal with being the human who must keep finding places and looking for stuff.

I have been a "who, what, where, when, why, how" professional since my first newspaper

job in 1962. The subject of the legend of a mysterious city in the jungle was not on my radar of usual beats—culture, politics, sports, and video portraits of known and unknown common people. A Lost City in the jungle seemed far-fetched to me, but it absolutely and steadily crept into my consciousness. In 2012, I ended 11 years of college teaching to spend as

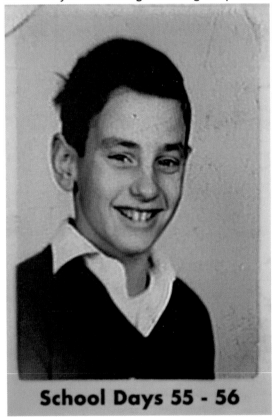

School Days 55 - 56

much time as possible on this wild goose chase adventure of jungle discovery.

My brain always wants to know where—as precisely as possible—when someone's telling a story. I know that they're telling it because of what happened to them. But I need to find out

where it happened before processing the effect it had or what the lesson was or how it changed their lives.

Of all the fundamental questions we journalists were taught, the "where" was huge for me.

All of this is a long way to explain why the thing that was most important to me about our jungle quest for the Lost City is that no human being had likely set foot in that exact spot on the earth for centuries. Looking down at nothing but dense forest from the helicopter and anticipating what was there was my first thrill. Setting foot on the ground was the big payoff for those moments and years in the ravines and in the mountains. And it was sacred. I've never experienced the spiritual and natural feelings that this spot in the jungle made me feel.

I guess that makes me a committed "where-guy."

We haven't stopped speaking about it since.

Our relationship as trusted friends and colleagues, with daily phone calls and e-mail correspondence, continues to this day. I don't think anything much happened leading to the discovery without our discussing and debating it.

Steve has a rare combination of abilities—a cinematographer and producer with scientific expertise and curiosity, consummate organizing skills and a no-nonsense personality. His dogged determination is tempered by his genuineness. We're a good match. My experience producing verité TV documentaries and videos, and my people-connections and skills complement Steve's many strengths. He has always been the jefe of the whole project.

Steve Elkins, aka in the Latin American press as "Dr. Helkins the American scientist," and I have known each other since 1975. He was an outdoor education instructor with the alternative Van Gorder-Walden School in Chicago and mostly living alone in a Wisconsin farmhouse. I was a TV documentarian based in Chicago. Steve and Janet, both from the Chicago suburbs, got married and in 1979, they headed to the West Coast to start a career selling hot dogs from a wiener mobile on Venice beach. His life's work morphed into a successful video rental business, PAL America, that serviced European TV producers. He became a skilled videographer who was in demand for decades. We had friends in common, were in touch occasionally, but never spoke about the Lost City until 1994.

Janet Elkins, successful in her own events business for decades, was dubious for many years, but never was heard a discouraging word. She always supported our cockamamie scheming to search for the Lost City, although she never let us forget that we were **"The Lost Boys."**

5

Honduras in search of what he believed was the Lost City of the Monkey God. His 1995 expedition journal *In Search of the Lost City of the Monkey Gods* articulated how impossible it was to negotiate the rivers and interior of the jungle.

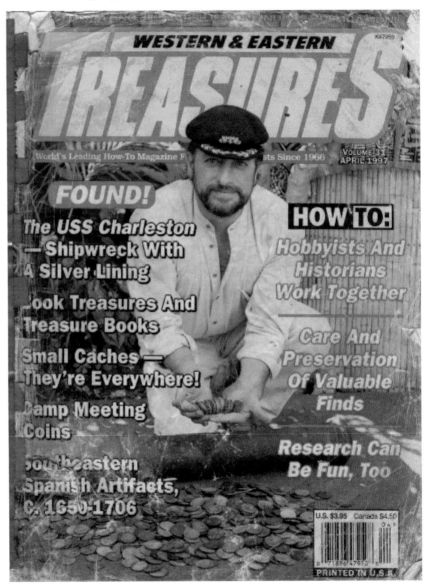

Steve Morgan, a self-identified captain, was the explorer in our group who originally pursued the Lost City. I met him through Steve Elkins in 1994. Captain Morgan was well-steeped in the legends of Ciudad Blanca by then. The three of us became business/explorer/documentary partners in 1995, shortly after the two of them returned from trekking and filming in the Mosquitia Jungle. They had been involved in initiating the discovery of **The Cave of the Glowing Skulls** near Catacamas. The skulls were radiocarbon dated and proved to be from 3,000 BC to 1,100 BC and were from a culture that couldn't possibly have been Maya or Aztec, the heights of which were millennia later.

Captain Morgan, in his 40s when I met him, grew up near St. Louis. He was ambitious, attractive, swashbuckling, convincing, conniving, and curious—always fascinated by science, history, and discovery. But his major motivator was money and that had a tendency to influence his judgment and straight-forward relationships.

By 2003, he had moved to the Philippines to search for buried treasures at the bottom of the ocean. He was moderately successful finding doubloons and stuff like that. He later suffered a series of strokes and couldn't speak. Sadly, he was incapable of participating in our 21st century expeditions to

Bruce Heinicke, a Missouri grade school backyard fossil-digging pal of Morgan's, lived in Eastern Honduras for ten years and married Honduran-born **Mabel** ("MAY-bell"). Bruce had one of the most colorful lives of anyone I've ever known. He was gruff, lived hard but had a good heart. Bruce was our Honduran connection—think "fixer." He'd been a quasi-legal drug cowboy character in the "wild west" days of the 1980s.

Mabel stuck by Bruce in Honduras, St. Louis, and Las Vegas, in sickness and in health, until his death in 2013. Mabel was instrumental in the revival of the project to search for Ciudad Blanca in 2009, after we had been stalled for several years.

Bruce's life, loves, and lucre were mercurial. He thrived on smoking, drinking, and telling real-life tales frequently involving saloons, guns, drugs, and dead guys. He genuinely cared about Mabel and their eight children. Their life was like a soap opera, replete with a devastating home fire. Bruce wound up in a coma for at least a month and then miraculously recovered. Bruce and I were opposites in many ways, but we got along fine and were able to focus on common goals for the years we teamed up.

Bruce died after realizing his dream of locating Ciudad Blanca with us in 2012, but he wasn't around when we went to the jungle in 2015. Mabel was in dire need of money and after our accomplishments had attracted worldwide attention, she tried to leverage her involvement into cash. She did get some financial help, but we couldn't come close to what she needed or expected, which eventually isolated her from the project. A long and exciting book could be written about their lives.

I'm a fourth-generation Chicagoan. When Steve Elkins first told me about the Lost City of the Monkey God in 1994, it captured me and never let up. The technical requirements and logistics involved in finding the Lost City were never my prime interests. It was living the story and then telling it on TV. I wanted the world to find out about the adventure, what fascinated us, how we stuck with it for 20 years, what we were able to do and not do, our cast of characters, and why the whole thing mattered in a larger historical and global context.

I have a unique history as a producer. Most of what I've done doesn't follow anyone else's template. That's always been the attraction for me and the viewers. I've had a pioneering TV/video life, using the tools to show the world and ordinary people as they are, not staged or manipulated in any way: **TVTV**—the first non-fiction portable video ever broadcast on television (1972-1977); *Image Union*—the first regularly scheduled series of truly independent video and film (1978-1988); the first new generation of video personality portraits on MTV News; *The 90's*—a groundbreaking PBS series with worldwide video correspondents (1989-1992); *Time Out*—a weekly informal sports show shot in a saloon set and incorporating unique sports music videos (1992-93); plus a few dozen documentaries, nearly all with quirky innovative twists.

My hands-on expertise with video equipment peaked in the last century. I have mostly been a hands-off organizer-producer-editor-director for a few decades. I taught as an adjunct professor from 2001-12 and founded the **Media Burn Independent Video Archive** in 2004—where we now have over 7,000 videos with about 3,000 of them online and free to view at **mediaburn.org**.

Before Our First Trip To Honduras

I started to believe we were chasing something that could be real when *Archaeology Magazine* published a story on the discovery of the **Cave of Glowing Skulls** in 1994.

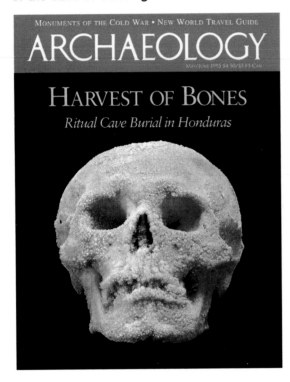

It became a scientific story with worldwide fascination. It was heralded as a genuine mystery, although indigenous people and gringos of the Olancho area had known about **Talgua Cave** for years. It was only a few miles from the end-of-the-road town of Catacamas but nobody who visited had ever examined the ledge where the skulls had been resting for thousands of years. That discovery was absolute proof for me that there was much more history and mystery in Northeastern Honduras.

Steve and I did as much research as possible to figure out where a city or civilization would be, if there really was one.

•

In 1995, we commissioned a **Japanese Earth Resources Satellite**—JERS—the best available then—to do a survey and gorgeous color photographic printout of a 15x20 mile area we had selected in the Mosquitia Jungle.

The area was our best guess about the location of a possible Lost City (or cities) in the uncharted and legendary Mosquitia.

We determined the location after reading piles of written historical accounts, deciphering maps, and doing video and telephone interviews with residents and experts. For several years, we did all we could to find out more about the myth and the realities.

On a TV production in New York in 1997, I paused for two days at the **New York Public Library**, doing research about the culture and myths connected to the Lost City in the Mosquitia. Nobody really had the answers.

A few of the possible truths were in some old sources from both the Latin American collection and Religion sections. (See **Notes.**)

When I was done, I didn't have many answers, but I was certain there must have been some truth to the centuries-old legends of Ciudad Blanca, Lost City of the Monkey God—perhaps with gold and effigies from a culture nobody had come in contact with for hundreds of years.

•

One of the most fascinating and convincing interviews we conducted was one that Steve Elkins did with **Sam Glassmire** in 1997, shortly before Sam died.

Sam was a wizened and credible man in his 80s, a prospector who took two months off his paid job to roam the Honduran jungle in 1959 in search of gold. He claimed he had found Ciudad Blanca.

Sam came back with many artifacts and an accurate hand-drawn map of his travels. He was the real thing, but it turns out he had gone to a location that was some 30 miles from our target.

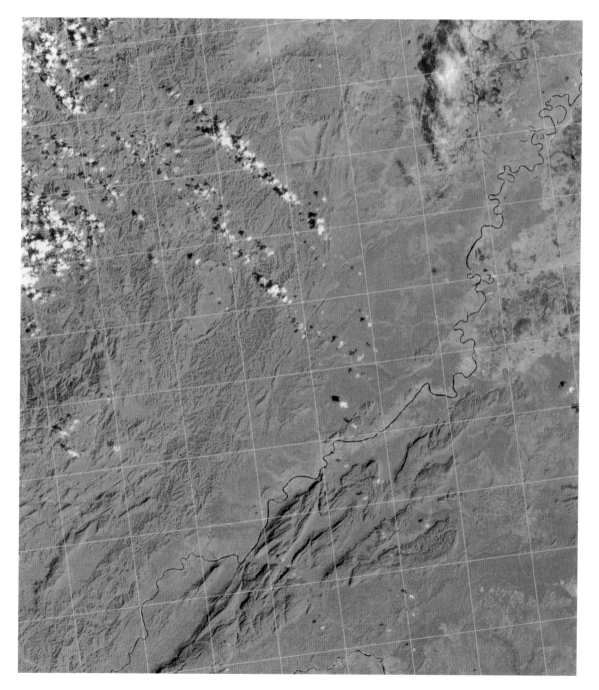

Using the satellite imagery from **JERS**, we identified a kidney-shaped and apparently uninhabited valley fifteen miles north of the **Patuca River** deep in the rainforest. Steve took the images to scientists—his local Pasadena connections at **Cal Tech**, and **NASA's Jet Propulsion Lab**. Steve met with the world expert on interpreting satellite data, **Dr. Ron Blom**.

Ron had used state-of-the-art satellite technology that led directly to the discovery of **The Lost City of Ubar** in the sands of the Arabian desert. The jungle is a very different situation, but we benefitted from his expertise in interpreting satellite data.

The data didn't determine anything definitive, but nobody disagreed with our guess that "our" valley could be a logical place for humans to live. We now know that there is only one way in and out at the location where two rivers flow through a narrow gorge (secure). It's in a mountainous region with a steep ridge around it (good protection), and possibly had its own microclimate, which would make the valley more hospitable than other parts of the vast tropical rainforest.

So we went to work, scheming, trying to attract media and money to our adventure.

Sukia Tara

We thought we needed a name for the Lost City that wouldn't get confused with Ciudad Blanca which, at the time, described several possible legendary locations. We came up with **"Sukia Tara,"** a compound word from the spoken language (**Pech**) of the indigenous people, a few of whom still live in the region of Eastern Honduras and Nicaragua. "Sukia" has been translated as "Medicine Man," referring to the leader who conducted ancient rituals. A fabled holy figure from local legends was known as **"Dama Sukia Tara."** Nobody had ever used "Sukia Tara," but it seemed credible to us.

With producer and graphics expert **Steve Naczinski**, we created a slick proposal for presentation to financial backers and media partners. Our careers as white-collar explorers hustling money and media lasted more than a year. Finding and documenting a lost ancient city in the jungle seemed to be a magnet for nuts of all kinds. But we did find genuine interest, from Japan to New Jersey, for documentary TV, serialization, magazine and fictionalization rights.

We thought we were on the cusp of major success. We had media and money partners with plane tickets all set to partner with us including Tokyo Broadcasting (set up by **Clarence Cross**), a group of investors from Miami with Latin American roots, British and German media conglomerates and a few others who had signed on pending approval of the government of Honduras. We were scheduled to bring eight people to a meeting with Honduran government officials in the capital, **Tegucigalpa**, on November 2nd, 1998.

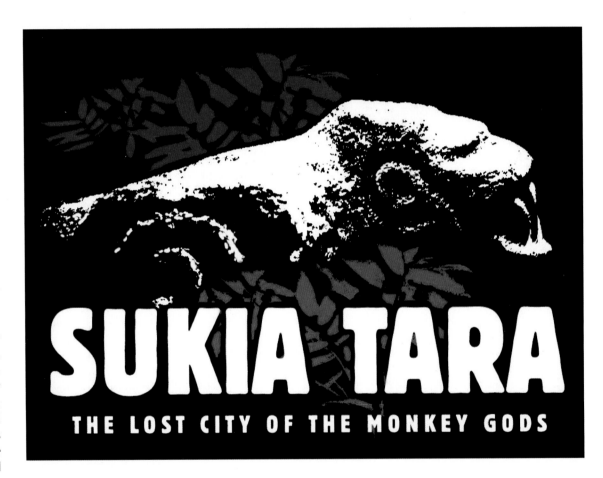

10

Hurricane Mitch

November 2nd, 1998, turned out to be four days after the worst hurricane in the history of Honduras struck land. As with many other setbacks, we half-jokingly attributed the events

Notwithstanding Mitch, I used my plane ticket and went to Tegucigalpa accompanied by my dear friend, **Eddie Becker,** a long-time videomaker and problem solver from Washington D.C. We were in the capital and then hung around **Soto Cano/Palmerol,** the

storm. Based on our satellite imagery, the village of a few hundred was the closest occupied place—15 helicopter minutes away from the valley we were calling Sukia Tara at the time.

Using our GPS, the U.S. military (**Joint Task Force Bravo**) agreed to do a flyover of the valley

to the wrath of the Monkey God—an integral part of the centuries-old **Ciudad Blanc**a legend.

The meeting was canceled, of course, a missed opportunity that wouldn't happen again for more than ten years.

joint U.S./Honduran military base.

There, **Colonel Jim Nelson** got interested in our story and arranged for us to join a medical mission to **Krausirpi**—a village of indigenous people that had been totally devastated by the

so we could photograph and shoot video. The military plan was to do a Medrete—a medical relief project—scheduled 10-15 days after I had already spent a week at the military base. That was plenty for me.

I flew back to Chicago and waited for the e-mail from Colonel Nelson to make the return trip, where I would do helicopter photo reconnaissance with **Trevor Gilchrest**, a professional still photographer Steve knew from Los Angeles. I brought my camcorder to shoot in the village and from the helicopter.

The information we gathered turned out to be valuable for Steve to confirm with the scientific team. After inspecting the video and photos they agreed we might very well be looking at a location where ancient people lived. Their reaction was reassuring and made the trips worthwhile.

•

Krausirpi and dozens of villages had been wiped out by the massive floods that followed Hurricane Mitch and unprecedented week-long tropical rains. These were indigenous tribal people living in virtual isolation. They scratched a living from the earth and the river. They had very little, but had survived that way for dozens of generations. Without help, it seemed like their villages weren't going to survive the hurricane's devastation.

When I returned to Tegucigalpa, I met with the publishers of the weekly English language newspaper, *Honduras Today*, and together we hatched a plan to raise money for the isolated villagers who needed basics like shelter and food. They could get wood to rebuild crude houses, but they couldn't get the nails to hold them together. And all their crops had been washed away by the floods. They needed to start over but had no seeds to replant. We committed to try to help them get seeds and nails.

When I got back to Chicago, I produced three television spots—a 30-second, a two-minute, and a five-minute spot—using the footage we

had shot in Krausirpi.

I wanted the spots to be broadcast as holiday fundraisers. **Bill Kurtis**, the consummate pro, was nice enough to do the voiceover. **Scott Jacobs** and IPA donated post-production. We raised several hundred dollars from broadcast on WGN-TV—a cable superstation at the time. It was shown in Miami, too, but we couldn't get enough stations or exposure to raise major money. Our Honduran partner was able to buy and send some seeds and nails to Krausirpi and other villages. But it was far less than we had hoped for.

After the hurricane, our Lost City efforts were stalled for years. Honduras was fighting for its very existence and a speculative archaeology expedition and documentary was a low priority. I kept in touch with Steve. He was doing well as a shooter for hire in Los Angeles. I was producing, mostly in Chicago, but spent time working on projects in New York, Colorado and San Francisco. Both of us had kids and families to take care of. There just wasn't much room in our lives for Lost City wild goose chases. Honduras remained in our brains, but not very actively.

SEEDS and NAILS

A Holiday Telethon for the survivors of Hurricane Mitch in Honduras

The Miracle Meeting

In 2009, **Mabel Heinicke**'s father died. She returned to Honduras to attend a Sunday mass in a Tegucigalpa church. It was there that she had what she insisted was a fated encounter with the newly-elected President of Honduras, **Porfirio Lobo Sosa**, and his right-hand man, Secretary of The Interior and Population, **Africo Madrid Hart**. Mabel all but forced Lobo to have a conversation about discovering Ciudad Blanca. He instructed Africo to make it happen. She then called Bruce in St. Louis from outside the church. President Lobo put Africo on the phone, who assured Bruce and Mabel that he would arrange the governmental details for an expedition to go the Mosquitia Jungle. She and Bruce called it the "Miracle Meeting."

Bruce got excited and called Steve who was gun-shy about starting out again on a high-risk jungle mission of discovery. He insisted on a bona fide letter from President Lobo committing to the expedition, including the exclusive rights for filming and all media. In typical Honduran style, the letter took nine months, but damned if it didn't arrive with official seals and hand signatures.

Steve and I had been in touch right after the Miracle Meeting. When the permission letter arrived, he called and the Lost Boys were back on the case to chase the legend of the Monkey God. We thought the official government letter would finally be a magnet for money to do the expedition. Our first priority was to use **LiDAR**, —**light detection and ranging**—an advanced laser imaging technology, to locate evidence of ancient remains in our identified sites.

The LiDAR could penetrate the jungle canopy, seeing the forest through the trees, and locate within a few centimeters any structures on the ground, such as roads, earthworks, pyramids or other manmade features.

In 2009, airborne LiDAR technology had succeeded in **Caracol**, Belize, to identify vast Mayan ruins which were unknown and unexplored by archaeologists after 25 years of on-the-ground work had been done. It was a stunning breakthrough.

We would use LiDAR from a low-flying airplane in a thick jungle location with no previous discoveries, something nobody else had done for archaeological purposes. We had an agreement for exclusive rights to document it in all media, while any discovery would remain the cultural patrimony of Honduras.

We had to admit that flying over the jungle with scientific instruments and using it to find stuff on the ground was something of a crapshoot. But how else are meaningful discoveries accomplished? It was a financial crapshoot, too—something on the order of a $250,000 investment. We tried asking everyone we knew, and many we did not, to raise the cash for an aerial survey of "our" valley.

Maury Kravitz, the guy who had spent personal millions trying to find Genghis Khan's tomb, explained to us that the payoff was in museum rights even more than media. But, he wasn't interested in supporting our venture.

I enlisted successful Chicago-based lawyer/agents **Todd** and **Brian Musburger** to work on the project. They were excited and tried hard, but we were unable to scare up the quarter-million after several months of hunting and fishing.

And Then Along Came Bill...

Santa Monica-based producer and director **Bill Benenson** decided to join Steve and me as a "Lost Boy" in 2010.

Bill was a first-class filmmaker who had produced several Hollywood features. He had also done some responsible documentaries. Bill and his wife, **Laurie**, were also generous donors to many progressive and ecological causes. His documentary *Dirt: The Movie,* released in 2009, had been an important revelation about the global abuse of soil, which endangered civilization on several levels. The movie was featured at many festivals.

Steve had worked with Bill as a videographer. They'd known each other for years. They had talked about the story and the legend of the Lost City in Honduras. Bill gave Steve some advice about how we could raise the money for the LiDAR expedition, but none of it panned out.

Finally, after close to a year, Bill decided to do it himself. He made a huge commitment to the project for his **Benenson Productions** in Santa Monica.

The original partnership was called **UTL Productions**, for "Under the LiDAR." Bill made the financial commitment, but Bill's close friend **Garry Spire** had a small stake as well.

Very soon after Bill had promised to underwrite or raise the necessary funds for the LiDAR expedition, I had my first meeting with him at a swank beach restaurant in Santa Monica. Bill, Steve and I talked for close to three hours. One of his first questions to me was, "Tom, do you plan to be part of this?"

I guess that after 18 years and having spent something like $30,000, I was slightly taken aback. I looked him straight in the eye and immediately replied, "Bill, you couldn't keep me away." So from that moment we were hooked together. After we'd been working together with Steve and others for two years, at another lunch by the beach, Bill volunteered that I would have the title Co-Producer on the documentary we were producing and he was directing.

14

Planning the Mission

In late 2011 we started calling the venture **A.K. Productions**, joking about the three of us (Bill, Steve and me) as *Alte Kakers*—defined by author **Leo Rosten** in *Joys of Yiddish*, *alte kakers* are crotchety, fussy, ineffectual old men. All three of us were past 60 (Bill and I were 70), teamed with much younger men and women in the project. Thankfully, it turned out we weren't ineffectual after all!

In the next couple years, I made seven trips from Chicago to Los Angeles/Santa Monica, and stayed mostly in Pasadena with Steve and Janet, most gracious hosts. Steve started his days around 5:30 AM. Mine frequently ended at 2 AM. Janet left for her real job at her own successful events company around 7:30 AM. I was out there usually for a week or ten days at a time. We met with Bill in Santa Monica at his office, along with the others at Benenson Productions. Spending time in LA was never a hardship. I have two sons and now a grandson plus lots of TV/video friends who had become Angelinos, many to their surprise.

The planning and prep phase for the LiDAR trip took about 16 months—from December 2010—until our group finally made it to Honduras on April 28, 2012. It included making arrangements with the Hondurans in **Tegucigalpa** and connecting with our crew who were going to be part of the LiDAR trip.

The key to it was the **National Center for Aerial Laser Mapping** (NCALM), a research organization funded by the **National Science Foundation** and headquartered at the **University of Houston** and the **University of California, Berkeley.**

We had several seemingly dead-end moments along the way, such as struggling for permission from the **U.S. State Department** to take LiDAR equipment out of the country. I was finally able to succeed with the help of the staff of Illinois Senator and then-Assistant Majority Leader **Richard Durbin.**

Everything we did was new to everyone. It was nerve-wracking to the extent that several times along the way, it seemed like the monkey gods had gotten the advantage. We were up against long odds just about every step of the way.

Steve remained at the center of it all. I was with him for many of the sessions that mattered, but he was at it every day, all over Los Angeles, Santa Monica, Pasadena, Oceanside and San Diego and points east.

We documented every stage of the process on video for use in our documentary. We knew that the discovery and the team involved were important enough to make a full-length documentary or several television episodes.

We planned to use the Honduran offshore Bay Island of **Roatan** as our headquarters. It would be about a 45-minute flight to our targets in the Mosquitia jungle in the Cessna with the LiDAR aboard.

Both the military and government said it would be safer locating in Roatan than on the mainland of Honduras where the murder rate was the highest of all the countries in the world at that time—thanks to narcotics traffic, gangs and widespread corruption.

LiDAR:

See the forest

Through the trees

For months, this was on the wall by my desk.
I never wanted to lose sight of what we were doing.

For us, it was to be two weeks—all expenses paid—at **The Parrot Tree,** a lovely Caribbean beach resort.

The plan was to do flights daily for ten days or so and record the process on video and still cameras. Although not everything went as planned, our first big group trip to Honduras revealed the presence of earlier human habitation in "our" valley, and it proved the value of LiDAR for archaeological purposes. We had already influenced the science of archaeology by making it a technological process rather than simply a human jungle expedition. Archaeologists and journalists called our airborne LiDAR discovery the most important technique since the first use of radiocarbon dating in the 1940s.

My Hopes And Fears

Far more than the LiDAR discovery, the ground-truthing in the jungle in 2015 was an emotional roller coaster. In the weeks and months before we all met at the Houston airport in 2015 and flew to **Tegucigalpa** on the way to **Catacamas** and the jungle, I didn't have the time or inclination to focus on my own feelings about the expedition. I bought the boots, clothes and camping gear, was in daily touch with Steve and was involved with Chris and the others, but I never was frightened.

Nothing terrible had ever happened to me. Fear of the external isn't my thing.

Yes, I'd had momentary flashes—on a shaky plane taking off, or getting thrown around by a wave and not being able to come up to breathe for ten seconds, or sitting in my wrecked car just after a kid crashed inches from me on the driver's side.

I know we're animals and the underlying and first reaction is fear.

But my most visceral fear has always been once-removed. It's that something awful—like getting dead—will happen to one of my kids and I'll have no control of the situation. (This continues into their 30s and 40s, but I was constantly and acutely aware of it when they were under ten.)

Even though dozens of people asked if I was scared during the months before we went to the jungle, I meant it when I said I wasn't—probably never smart enough to be scared when there's something real to be scared of.

I WAS afraid that I wouldn't be in good enough physical condition to do what most of the others could do. I was older than all of them. But that was about slowing down, resting, or stopping, not about life and limb.

Let me back up for a moment—I've never thought I was like everyone else. I've lived my life as an exception, not intentionally as many have believed—including teachers, wives and shrinks—but just because I found out when I was six or so that I WAS an exception. It seemed like I've always thought and felt and done things nobody else did. Of course, you never know what it's like to be inside anyone else's head, but as a kid, when others talked about being scared, I wasn't—not by horror stories, movies, monsters, animals or "dangerous" situations.

Hopes? In this case, I knew that I wanted to find something nobody else had ever seen. And I hoped we could show it and explain it to the world. Rich and Famous? For me, personally, I hoped to get recognition from people I knew — and some I didn't know—for having stuck with a mission and dream and grown with it for 20 years. It was an accomplishment to be a major part of a team that made a meaningful historic discovery—and for me and millions of others worldwide, it's only REAL if it's on TV. Aside from that, we just wanted to have some fun.

My history and expertise is organizing and creating revealing video and television, telling the human stories behind events. It's unabashedly honest, spontaneous, and rings true, showing how people live, relate, emote, and perceive their experiences.

Yes, Steve and I spent a few moments entertaining thoughts of fame, but that has never been my primary motivation. Why would I have spent a life making hundreds of documentaries and TV shows about other people if I really wanted them to be about me? Dozens of times, we'd leave my laugh or my reaction because I really was there and part of what makes it fun is to be spontaneous as it's happening. That's not trying to get famous—for me it's just a reminder that I was integral in making it happen. When I hear it or see it on the screen, I DO like it because it reinforces the cool part of doing what I've done as a producer for almost 50 years.

The same thing goes for hoping to get rich. I always thought there was a tiny possibility that finding the Lost City would get us some money. It hasn't. The video crew, the British jungle guys, the archaeologists, the LiDAR experts, our fixer, the drivers, pilots, assistant producers, etc. all earned money working on this project.

Steve and I got plane tickets, lodging, and some snake gaiters. In fact, in the early years between 1994 and 1998, we spent something like $30,000 of our own money to keep the project going. I would love to get that back—I could use it now!—but that was never what was driving us. We were along for the ride of our lives, eventually made possible primarily by Bill Benenson's involvement and cash plus our own perseverance.

•

PART TWO: CHRONICLES 2012 - THE LIDAR SEARCH

#1 How Do You Look For A Lost City?
Tuesday, April 18, 2012
Corn Island, Nicaragua

I've spent seven on and off sunny days and nights in my beach bungalow on **Corn Island** lying in wait for the oft-postponed rendezvous with our long-frustrated leader, **Steve Elkins**, and the rest of our team.

We will be nestled comfortably in an all-suite resort, on the island of **Roatan.** A Cessna with expert occupants and million-dollar instrumentation is being flown from Houston to the Bay Islands—two-days of flying. It will

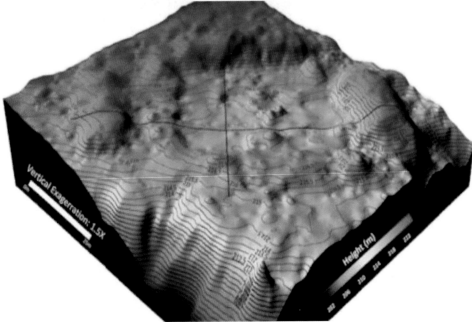

make twice-daily forays over the **Mosquitia Jungle** in the middle of green-nowhere at less than 2,000 feet above the sites we have designated. We chose the sites based on the original 1998 satellite data Steve and I bought, my flyover in 1998, some newly acquired hi-res satellite images and a lot of intuitive guesswork aided by advisors from the **Jet Propulsion Laboratory** in Pasadena, CA.

Each day, when the plane returns to base, the **LiDAR** data it records will be input to computers at our island HQ and some sophisticated process of rendering will ensue.

We are working with expensive research contractors at **The National Center for Airborne Laser Mapping** (NCALM) in Houston and Berkeley.

LiDAR is an optical remote sensing technology that can measure the distance to and the physical components of a target by illuminating the target with beams of light—jillions of pulses from lasers that then bounce back to an onboard computer.

Our guys say that these flyovers can yield results that show structures, roads, and other three-dimensional information down to a few inches in size—assuming there's no raindrops for the sensors to be distracted by.

What it's all about is that these laser showers—or at least a few of them—are able to penetrate the trees of the jungle canopy and "see" what's down there. Getting in there on foot is nearly humanly impossible—it has killed plenty of seekers—and even if you were able to penetrate some of the densest jungle in the Americas you would almost definitely not be able to find any evidence of buildings or civilization through the miles of thousand-year-old growth. And getting back out wouldn't be much fun.

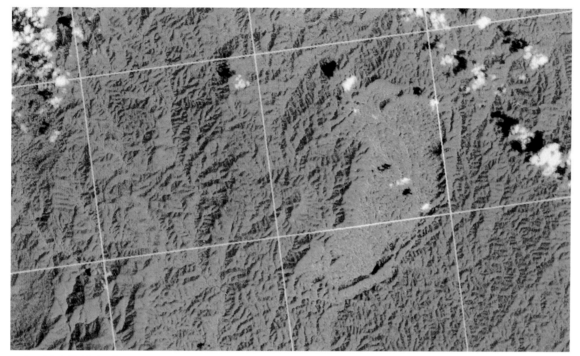

So this LiDAR is the way to go. It's not a brand new technology. It has had military, mapping, resource determination, and many other uses. But only in the last two years has it been a tool for archaeological research.

Part of the reason is that not very many people or institutions have been able to muster the money to do it. Plus, only a few airborne LiDAR rigs exist and there is a golden rule at work—those looking for gold or oil come first.

We've identified four target sites, all within about 25 miles of each other. Some are more likely to have ancient stuff on them than others.

But the most exciting one—our Target #1 or **T1**, the one I call **"Elkins Valley"**—is kidney-shaped and seems to be surrounded by a continuous ridge about 800-1,000 feet above the floor of the valley. It's about three miles long and a mile or so wide. Talk about

a needle in a haystack. (This is just about the same size as Corn Island, my vacation spot—a speck in the Caribbean that is less than 200 miles southeast of the target. So I have a sense of the proportion of the site.)

"Elkins Valley" has been examined closely by satellite interpreters, geology experts, and anthropologists who seem to agree that it's a logical spot for humans to have lived in some 800 to 1,000 years ago. It's a good altitude for people to live in, grow stuff and breathe. It would be relatively easy to defend from outsiders who would have to scale the ridges and who could be seen from above. And it also has some interesting meteorological possibilities in that it might have its own more temperate weather system—microclimate—compared to the stifling heat and humidity of

the surrounding jungle. Probably the valley's most important feature is the river system. It looks like there are two rivers running through it, joining near the center. Civilizations ("cities") usually grow next to running water. And these are pretty good size rivers that flow down to the sea some 40-50 miles to the east.

Another notable phenomenon is that our other target sites are located in protected areas, in almost a straight line, within 20 miles of Elkins Valley.

This would tend to corroborate the theory of Honduran-American archaeologist **George Hasemann**, who died young in the 1990's. He wrote papers theorizing that there isn't

just one "Lost City," but rather an extensive complex of places which were built around and near a central hub that had the largest buildings, temples, commercial centers, etc. Not hard for us moderns to understand the city/suburb configuration.

So we shall see. Once we get some LiDAR results from flyovers starting in our **T1** valley, we'll determine what our next target will be. We have enough money to spend 6-10 days doing this fly-fuel-scan-render-feedback-fly fuel-scan again process.

The money will be flying out of the coffers of **Bill Benenson**'s UTL Productions—something like $15,000 a day for the NCALM contract that includes the plane, LiDAR rig and the engineers; another few thousand a day for food and lodging for our distinguished group; another couple thousand a day for the for the video guys and their equipment; and then there's **Bruce Heinicke**, and your scribe (moi), plus our leader, Steve. Also in the budget are the inevitable Honduran shakedowns along the way.

Bill himself isn't likely to attend the festivities. He is now at a film fest in China with a film he co-produced and co-directed, *Dirt: The Movie* (2009)—very well-done and responsible.

The last time I saw Bill was at an elegant party he threw in Santa Monica for a few Hondurans flown in for the occasion and about 25 of his pals/potential investors, mostly from Santa Monica.

At the party Steve and **Virgilio Paredes Trapero**—head of the **Honduras Institute of History and Anthropology** (IHAH)—gave clear, fascinating, informal talks right after dinner. Steve ran down a bunch of the history, the legend, what we did in the 90's, how LiDAR works and thanked the government of Honduras for its wonderful support and collaboration.

Virgilio isn't an anthropologist. He's a politically-connected ambitious 40-something who says he has a bunch of degrees. His most memorable remark was, "I know you are going to find the Lost City. I'm just worried about what will happen after that. We will need to protect it from anyone who might want to get in for whatever reason."

Think larceny. Of course, the deal in the written contract signed by Honduran Secretary of the Interior, **Africo Madrid Hart**, Virgilio,

Steve, and Bruce specifies that every physical object will remain the cultural patrimony of the Honduran people. President **Porfirio Lobo Sosa** has said straight out that he wants this discovery project to succeed, both to open a new world-shaking historical tourist site, and no less significantly, to change the current global image of Honduras as the Murder Capital of the World—which, per capita, it is by a large margin over any other country. He says he has heard the legends of the Lost City in Mosquitia—not far from his own birthplace—for his whole life and is fascinated to find out what's there.

That this whole thing is happening at all is because of the convergence of a remarkable, near-perfect storm:

• The current **Honduran government**—less than two years since it took power by coup d'etat—has a personal and national vested and public interest in making it happen and doing what it can to facilitate it. Honduras is so screwed up by a history of rape and pillage by the US and other countries, by the omnipresence and influence of the drug cartels and the violence and fear they bring, and by the "regular" mañana culture of inefficiencies, bribery, and tremendous poverty.

• The advent of **LiDAR technology**, which has been well-documented (in The New York Times, Archaeology Magazine, and academic journals) for its unprecedented success in finding amazing stuff at a site in Belize which had been excavated by professors and students for 25 years. Using LiDAR, researchers found huge structures and features that they had no previous knowledge of despite their being just a few hundred yards from their thick jungle digs. LiDAR is a game-changer.

• The **Benenson Factor**. This is not penny-

ante poker. Somebody's got to step forward as a believer. Bill has to both have the shekels and the vision to see that this could be major, both from a history/science/where-we-came-from perspective and, to be sure, as a high-risk investment—more than $300,000 cash—with a potentially big return. The documentary, TV series, books, museum shows, a novel, a movie, each with major global distribution all dance in Bill's head—and ours. Along with the recognition that he—and we—made the impossible possible.

Without all three of these, none of it would be happening. I might have been in Corn Island on the beach for a few days—I like it here—but I never would have been en-route to this adventure into the unknown. It's kinda like Indiana Jones without the violence or fighting.

•

Next, I hope, you will be hearing from me based on **Roatan**, still another Caribbean island paradise.

I have also been doing some serious thinking about the paradoxes of paradises—but that's for some other venue and some other time.

#2 Go - No Go?
Monday, April 23, 2012
Corn Island, Nicaragua (still)

Last Friday, April 20, 2012 was well on its way to becoming Good Friday for all of us Lost Boys.

All the permits were finally cool—or the fuel and for the Honduran military copter to take us to plant the GPS boxes, and permission for our Cessna to fly and land in Roatan and in **Catacamas** for the fuel, to fly over the Mosquitia Jungle twice a day at under 1,200 feet, and then fly back to Roatan.

Steve was just "thisclose" to locking in the air and ground arrangements—for the flights to Roatan—LA to Houston to Roatan (party of 7 or 8), plus getting Bruce Heinicke from St. Louis-HOU-RTB, maybe even a little early to meet me. I'm making my own ever-changing reservations on **Taca** (aka Caca) with huge help from my interpreter, **Costanza Lenner Mellerio**. I'm a couple hundred miles away, but it would be far easier and not much more expensive to get there nonstop from Toronto.

Bruce and Steve were imagining themselves with a cocktail on the Caribbean after all the craziness of the past three months of starts and stops – the governmental yesses then nos, the unexpected hurdles from Houston, the U.S. State Department, the Honduran Aviation authority, the military, and all the rest. Finally two days ago, it was all set—the 17-year chase will actually be happening—YES!

But, Nooooooo! About 2 o'clock PDT, in flies another black swan—just when it was finally a real GO and Houston was ramping up the computer, the rendering software, GPS ground triangulation boxes and so on, Bruce finds out by email two things:

• The military doesn't have the budget to pay for the out-of-pocket maintenance costs to plant the three GPS boxes. We'll need to do that ourselves as triangulation is crucial so renderings can be as accurate as possible. Cost to the project for that little hustle is about $5,000. Not what we expected, but it is a cash cost. "OK," says Elkins, probably after checking it out with Bill and/or Garry Spire, Bill's pal and minority partner.

• And—this one's a heartbreak—the whole well-developed and agreed upon plan to get the fuel to refuel our plane at Catacamas on the mainland was up for grabs. The deal Steve and Bruce had worked out was to truck the fuel some 100 miles from the capital, **Tegucigalpa**, to the refueling spot at Catacamas. Now the government says there is a "security problem" trucking it in. They want to bring the fuel for the Cessna to **La Ceiba** via helicopter. A helicopter flying a gasoline tank more than 120 miles—how is that not a "security problem?" Sounds like a bomb! And quick math yields an estimate of at least $10,000 and maybe a whole lot more for the maintenance cost of the military's probably well-worn helo. Highway robbery—or maybe chopper chutzpah. This is not a simple question of our closing our eyes and "just pay what they're asking" —It's significant cash. And a monkey wrench in our operating efficiency. We know by now that when you do "The Fix" in Honduras, it doesn't always stay fixed. They're on the Pay Now - Pay More Later Plan. The deal-making doesn't seem to get it fixed for good the way it usually does in, say, Chicago. And the only way to blow the whistle on the guy who has stretched his paws out too far is by having him told by a big boss to shut up or he'll be taken care of in a different way. This is the Wild West.

•

This just in...
EMAIL UPDATE from Steve Elkins (to the entire crew)
0800 Saturday morning, April 21
Pasadena, CA
All government permits (both USA and Honduras) have been received. As of yesterday afternoon all logistics were set in place. The plan is to leave either Wednesday, Thursday or Saturday at the latest. The trip will last between one and two weeks depending on how fast the LiDAR scans can be done.

Because of the anti-narco policy in effect in Honduras, the sale of aviation fuel is restricted and not available where we need it. To overcome this obstacle we have received a special permit to buy and transport the fuel to the airport the LiDAR plane will use. We also made an arrangement to have the fuel trucked to the location by secure ground transport.

Late yesterday I was informed that the fuel must be transported by helicopter and the cost to do this is unknown – to me this spells shakedown. This is a real zinger as it could easily cost tens of thousands of dollars to do this. I have had similar problems while organizing this production and hope to have it worked out over the weekend. So once again, please stand by for a day or two.

By the way, the variable departure dates are due to not knowing when the fuel will be delivered as it makes no sense to be there without it. The ground transport people said they would have it in place by Thursday – but that was before I got the notice about having to heli it in for a mysterious cost.
Such is life in the third world.
--Steve

So, as of this morning, Monday, April 23, Commander Steve and Fixer Bruce were finally able to take care of business. Hallelujah! It's nice to be the king—at least the boss of just about everyone in the government in a small country. Our Honduran Heavy, Cabinet Minister Africo Madrid Hart, is the man who can.

•

FYI, here's a February 2010 online blog providing some political background on Africo Madrid:

*"...Cabinet Minister África Madrid is a long-time political activist in the National Party... As early as 1994, he became visible by attacking the sitting Liberal Party President **Carlos Reina** of abuse of authority and misuse of public funds, for his intervention to end a banana workers' strike. In the last Nationalist Party administration, Madrid served as vice-minister of Labor. Perhaps equally pertinent to his position in the Lobo Sosa cabinet, though, is that Madrid rose to be the director of the National Party—Madrid is, clearly, a major political operative in the Nationalist Party, and it is not surprising that he has a place in the Lobo Sosa cabinet.*

What may be surprising is that he did not end up with the post of Secretary of State (Cancillería or Relaciones Exteriores), which press reports indicated he was pushing to receive. Indeed, in the transition team of Lobo Sosa, Madrid coordinated the External Relations team, and was quoted in the press expansively commenting on the future goals of that ministry, in a way that seemed appropriate for the next occupant of that post.

*But in the end External Affairs went to another—**Mario Canahuati** who, in addition to his role as a vigorous defender of the coup d'etat of 2009, promoted the idea that the economic sector could withstand international pressure, and was a major rival of Lobo Sosa's in the primary campaign for the National Party nomination. More pertinent, perhaps, to this decision... is Canahuati's experience as a former ambassador to the US, the primary focus of Honduran foreign policy now and for the foreseeable future. That leaves África Madrid trying to deal with the lingering effects of the polarization of Honduran civil society."*

By this afternoon, it really IS a GO!!

Steve has booked all the plane tickets and rooms. Houston is ready. We will rendezvous on Saturday, April 28 in Roatan.

We've been on this case for 17+ years. Only the Monkey God knows what fate will befall us in the next two weeks! Stay tuned.

#3 Live From Roatan
Sunday night, April 29, 2012
Roatan, Bay Islands, Honduras

All equipment and people arrived, made it through customs and bussed to the Parrot Tree Resort with help from Bruce and our Roatan expediter, **Lomar Martinez**, 27, of Ana Caribe.

•

Arriving en masse from Houston via United, on time and on budget—except for the exorbitant baggage fee—were:

Commander **Steve Elkins**, flanked by audio/utility **Mark Adams**, and cameraman **Steve Graham** from LA.

Michael Sartori, senior engineer from **NCALM** in Houston.

Writer **Doug Preston** from Santa Fe.

Juan Carlos Fernandez Diaz and **Abhinav Singhania** from NCALM

Roberto Ysais, still photographer from Los Angeles

The Parrot Tree Resort is in a gorgeous bay setting—a two-year-old multi-million-dollar property with magnificent posh rooms. Actually, they're kitchenettes with bedroom, bathroom and a "kitchen," with stove, microwave, fridge, and housewares. Dark wood, granite, nothing on the cheap. At least $350/night rack rate. Our 11 units are each something like $200 for UTL. Good deal for everyone.

At Sunset we went down to the **Palapa Bar and Grill** where we had a beer or two and then early dinner, all of us together at two outdoor tables. Lobster, lessons on the science of how LiDAR works, discussion of where the LiDAR Cessna and its pilot, **Chuck Gross**, are—Key West in some tough weather—followed by a

serious discussion about what the drill was to be today:

Early AM charter straight wing from Roatan to meet the helicopter in **San Pedro Sula**.

We have three objectives:
• Get two additional GPS units functioning on the ground so that they can send signals to the LiDAR plane's onboard computer while it's recording data on its flying missions. This enhances the data collected by making the navigation component more accurate and, I think, shortens the time it will take to get full readings. In addition to here in Roatan, the other locations will be at **Catacamas** and **Dulce Nombre de Culmi.**

• Set up data collection on a laptop which will gather our daily data so it can then be sent on to be processed asap. In charge of the data wrangling is **"Mango"** aka **Marvin Hernandez,** our Honduran jack of all trades—a former national football star and coach and the brother of **Mabel Heinicke,** Bruce's wife.

• If possible and practical, do a pass-by in the helicopter over **T1** and others—time, weather, fuel, and pilot permitting—just to see what they look like from eyeballs and video.

•

Decision making at dinner revolved around the reality that there is room for only four bodies in the helicopter in addition to the government pilot. Although earlier in the week we expected to be supplied a Huey-type Honduran military chopper, it was busy today on "security business." Think drug-busting. So, for this first mission, we have the smaller personal helicopter assigned to **Africo Madrid,** the Cabinet minister, senior government official, and the guy who signed the contract with Steve and Bruce in 2011.

So who goes?

Bruce Heinicke signed up to be responsible for Africo's helicopter so he must go; Mango, the only one who knows the location of his uncle's farm where the GPS will be set up near Dulce and will need to learn how to deal with uploading data during flying days; Steve Graham, to shoot in the helicopter with a smallish camera and document the day's proceedings; and one of the LiDAR technicians to actually set up the GPS.

When Bruce filled out the form as to who would be on the helicopter—a government requirement communicated by **Virgilio**

Paredes—he listed Michael Sartori, the senior member of the LiDAR team. But after some give and take, hemming and hawing, and measuring the up and downsides, Michael felt that Juan Carlos would be better because he could easily do the technical setup and he could explain the job to Mango who doesn't speak English.

Seemed logical, but Bruce was stuck on how Michael was listed, his passport number submitted and that he needed to go.

Commander Elkins made the decision—Juan Carlos would go. He would become Michael and use Michael's passport. Juan and Michael are both of dark complexion, about the same height, and—sorry—can both pass for geeks. Juan Carlos memorized the passport data and carried both his and Michael's in case he had to come clean.

Steve said, "Hey, we'll take that chance. They won't care." Bruce was pretty silent about it but was obviously stewing inside as he is wont to do.

Next came the evening briefing session in Command HQ, aka Steve's room. All but Bruce were there. Steve paid out per diems in cash for the first seven days and did a half hour-plus no-nonsense rundown of why we were here, what not to tell anyone, a look at recent high-resolution satellite photos of the three target areas, plus a lesson in settlement archaeology from a 1997 video interview with George Hasemann who ran the IHAH for 16 years until his death in 1998.

The capper of the evening was the video interview with prospector **Sam Glassmire** that Steve shot with him in 1997. Many in the group didn't know most of Steve's show-and-tell, but they were clearly impressed and with that knowledge, their involvement ratcheted up a few notches.

#4 A New Dawn, A New Day – A New Story

Monday, April 30, 2012
Roatan, Bay Islands, Honduras

This morning we got up around 5:30 and left for a 30-minute ride to the airport at 6:00. Nine of us in the van, including a still slightly grumbly Bruce, three video cameras, a bunch of tripods and a few bags of gear.

Nobody had a cup of coffee until we got to the airport.

Long and short, the pilot and charter arrived. Bruce, Juan Carlos, Mango and Steve got onboard after we paid a few bucks each for the

Dulce, it turned out that Mango couldn't recognize Tio's farm from the air.

So they landed on a soccer field where they were greeted as stars by the locals. They all prepared for a car ride to the farm with Mango's pal, some 20 miles down the dirt road. But they managed to figure out where it was and it only took a few more minutes in the air to get there and set up the GPS.

When they stopped for fuel, I was finally able to reach Bruce on his cell around 4:00 pm – some 90 minutes before they HAD to be back in Roatan in order to land in the daylight. All was cool—cooler—at that point. Bruce and Juan Carlos had apparently disagreed earlier about whether to "get the job done" at Catacamas. Seems it was settled de facto by the helicopter

intra-Honduran airport fees and they cleared security. Mark, Steve, and Roberto got on the tarmac to document the departure. Crew and pilot boarded and left for the set-up journey.

The mission's first stop was **San Pedro Sula** where "our" helicopter arrived for a pre-arranged rendezvous with Virgilio Paredes Trapero (head of the IHAH). And who shows up? **Sr. Africo Madrid** himself, who "loaned" us his governmental helicopter for the day. Africo has steadfastly been the chief advocate for our project and get-things-done official from the start.

In San Pedro Sula, Africo took our crew to his private club, introduced them to his family, paid for the fuel, had photos taken with all the guys and then he and his boyhood pal Virgilio went on their way back to Tegucigalpa.

After lunch at the Christopher Columbus resort in Trujillo, our guys took off in Africo's helicopter and headed for **Dulce Nombre de Culmi**—the name probably has more letters than the town has people. But flying over

pilot who decided it was time to start heading back to San Pedro, the base for Africo's heli, and that the more than 6 hours flying time for the day was enough for all concerned. They took off to drop the guys in Roatan.

Mission accomplished? Well mostly, except for a couple of details like not setting up the GPS in Catacamas or testing the data-sending from Dulce and whatever scars remained from the conflict between Bruce and Juan Carlos. (Bruce's territorial belligerence toward Juan Carlos had actually started several days before.)

But it was a clear, bright sunny flying day and Steve Graham got some lovely shots of rural Honduran people and land. Not sure yet if there was video of Africo and his family greeting and embracing Bruce, but the day's events are probably pretty well-documented in his more than three hours of video. I saw a quick playback driving back to the ranch. It definitely looks like there's a sequence of setting up GPS, which is, after all, what this 11-hour, ~ $15,000 day was mostly about.

We greeted the returning crew as they arrived in Roatan airport before dark. They were pumped and exhausted after a day they wouldn't forget for many reasons.

Back at the ranch, Mark shot a bunch of video mostly with Steve along with some Parrot Tree beauty shots. Roberto never stopped looking, clicking and enjoying his artful digital still photos. The rest of us swam, schmoozed and schemed a bit.

Our reality tonight: Still no LiDAR plane! Mañana. Damn well better be. Our pilot, Charles Gross III, has had a couple nights in Key West, waiting out stormy weather. We need him to show up. We're already a day behind our schedule for tracking that Lost City.

•

#5 Waiting—Still And Again—For The Cessna
Monday night, April 30, 2012
Roatan, Bay Islands, Honduras

Commander Elkins had some hard decision-making to do. First, finalizing the financial/contractual arrangements with Bruce Heinicke. Based on their understanding from two years ago, a paper had to be signed. Bruce got what he wanted and his legacy is now confirmed in a written agreement for Bruce's compensation, current and future with UTL that Steve executed with approval from Bill Benenson.

(Unlike Bruce, I have no written financial contractual deal with UTL. Although I wrote a draft of one last January to be granted a percentage of Steve's 49% ownership interest, I am relying 100% on the Steve's verbal commitment that I will have an appropriate long-term equity participation as well as an equitable share of revenue, if and when the project generates cash to the principals beyond the costs. I absolutely trust Steve to honor that commitment.)

The second problem was about video quality. Elkins and Steve Graham looked at footage from today's plane and helicopter mission. It was seriously disappointing – technically, storytelling-wise, and as an indication of the video shooting-to-come for the days ahead. The Commander had to make a very difficult call. He and I discussed it at some length and he decided around 7 pm. The fallout will come tomorrow—Tuesday morning. Tough stuff—but Elkins, as the best shooter in camp, couldn't and wouldn't tolerate or accept anything less than what he knew needed to be done.

The Commander's decision about limiting what Steve Graham shoots will have ramifications. But with the mission-managing support Elkins has, from Doug, Mark and me, it will free him up to shoot more and delegate some of the producing as required. He shoots great and the video must reflect his first-class capabilities.

Meanwhile, **STILL NO LiDAR PLANE!**

Stuck in Key West for night #3. Pilot Charles Gross had better make it here by Tuesday or it's May Day in more ways than one for him and his company.

Let's just assume he will make it to Roatan by afternoon. I was a little outspoken about the situation at our morning meeting, but the frustration of 17+ years on the project, the astronomical expenses of waiting, the belief that the LiDAR "research" unit and its people were operating under a different set of realities and understanding of time and priorities

34

than we are as documentarians, stakeholders and Lost City seekers all contributed to my expressed frustrations. I asked the three Houston techs and it turns out that no one has ever flown with Gross. He is a substitute pilot - a complete unknown even to the NCALM guys here. I had the audacity to ask, "Who's the boss of him?" in public. It didn't make me popular. But it was, and still is, a question that needs to be answered. Nobody says that he should fly in unsafe weather, for sure. All that is important is that he (and everyone) understands the realities: who they're contracted with and then do his damnedest to get that Cessna wheels down in Roatan, Honduras – which is less than a 4-hour flight from his current three-night stand-still in Florida.

•

The Big Picture: We are more than 24 hours —more like 48—behind schedule. The video isn't a story told well enough at this point. If we have to re-shoot at some of yesterday's helicopter locations we will. But, we are a strong and professional group. We know there is a Lost City out there somewhere. And we'll know a helluva lot more about it in the next 48 hours. By the time **Garry Spire** and/or Bill arrive in a few days, we will have made necessary adjustments and know lots more than we do right now.

And when the IHAH archaeologist arrives tomorrow, our whole crew understands the drill —we're doing a survey of the Mosquitia - as much of the area ecology, forestation, archaeology, flora and fauna as time and money permits. We are documenting the process of using this remarkable new LiDAR technology. No more info for him. He is not seen as trustworthy by the Hondurans who trust us and with whom we have made our arrangements. The internal Honduran politics seem to be operating constantly and we can't possibly know the nuances.

Meanwhile, Bruce wound up satisfied with his long-term deal and Mango's cash payment. Roberto continues to shoot terrific stills. The three Houston guys continue to wait. And I—who did spend a few hours on the computer dealing with two Chicago-based situations—continue to be 100% supportive of Commander Elkins and making our project as successful as possible.

No matter what else might be happening, my ethos is steadfast and similar to Bruce's: "Do everything that it takes to get the job done and done right." That will continue, as will the strengths and weaknesses of all of us residing in beautiful Parrot Tree. Personally, I just hope— for a number of reasons—that our stay will not carry too far into the merry month of May.

We now have a second vehicle. It was used for shopping and later a dinner trip by a few. Juan Carlos, Abhinav, Preston and I were snorkeling for a while today. It was nice to see stuff under the water, but viewing the jungle by LiDAR will be way more productive. Looks like that will be possible on Wednesday at the soonest.

#6 "The Plane, The Plane!"
Tuesday night, May Day, 2012
Roatan, Bay Islands, Honduras

YES!! We got word at 7 AM that pilot **Chuck Gross** was leaving Key West shortly. It radically changed the mood in camp. After all, we got nothing if we don't have LiDAR results – whatever they turn out to be.

At a leisurely breakfast, Doug captivated the group with background stories about the real-life drama of **The Monster of Florence**, a 2008 *New York Times* best-seller he wrote after living in Italy for four years with his family.

At the airport, **Jose Izcoa Ramas** the rep from IHAH, was greeted by Steve, Bruce and me, with Steve Graham, Mark and Roberto to document it. He arrived about 10 AM, a 50-ish Honduran who seems petty innocuous looking and ready for a pleasant six-day stay at the beach. It seemed he didn't speak or understand English, but he is never supposed to know anything from us—even that there's a Lost City involved, much less what we find. But Mark Adams seems pretty certain that he understands English quite well.

So far I'm not sure of that, but we've been warned about him and his political loyalties by Virgilio, but that could be company politics. Until Virgilio returns from Philadelphia and the Mayan Exhibit where President Pepe Lobo will be at the opening, we gotta be cautious about Jose and what he sees and hears. We mostly shunt him off to the side to work on his maps and papers.

Chuck Gross, the pilot, called around 11 AM. He was in Grand Cayman refueling and they wouldn't take the credit card from the University of Houston. He didn't have $540 and only by getting them to charge it to Steve Elkins' credit card was another weird Houston administrative loose-end avoided. Who could think up all these possible fiascos and stumbling blocks? We just need to deal with them as they pop up.

Now we had over two hours before plane would arrive. No reason to go back to Parrot Tree. A few of us went to a tipico restaurant with Bruce to eat. We couldn't go to Island Saloon because it was closed for May Day, a Honduran national holiday that's equivalent to our Labor Day. Doug Preston and I stopped at Claro to deal with our cell phones.

Chuck was thrilled to finally get out of Key West. He told of the 5 inches of rain that fell the night before he left and 3 inches that fell the day before that (Sunday). Chuck says that he took some pictures of the ducks on the pond-like runway. He has years in the military, finding and reporting data for targets for use in the wars in Mideast. He got a thorough briefing his first night on what we're doing here, what it looks like from our sophisticated satellite images of the jungle targets, an actual shot I took from a US military helicopter in 1998, the stakes we're playing for and why it all matters. Steve made it clear to him that when he's in the air to keep his eyes open for suspicious or curious stuff and to note the readings. Our targets probably won't turn up many (if any) people, but his experience with scanning is the right stuff for what we're doing.

With plenty of time and proper permissions, thanks to Bruce and our local expediter Lomar we had two video cameras with Steve Elkins and Steve Graham shooting and Roberto shooting stills ready for the arrival of the Cessna.

When Chuck Gross landed, customs for the gear was taken care of without a hitch or need for the standard quarantine.

Steve got shots of Chuck and the plane, followed by a sequence with our seven military guards with their machine guns, marching and protecting this little plane on the runway. They get a week's pay for every day they guard the precious LiDAR and Cessna. And they got into it – they've been waiting around for three nights in a hotel next to airport for this very moment.

Pilot Chuck came inside, greeted and meeted, went to the baño, and got ready for takeoff to Trujillo for Juan Carlos to put the GPS on a tripod that came in the plane and then gas up for Wednesday, the first day of flying and scanning. Elkins and company got shots of getting in and taking off. About 3:30, the whole gang piled in a van for the 25-minute drive to Parrot Tree. Archaeologist Jose Ramas was with us and checked in.

about the technology, the timing, and what we can expect logistically. Explanations of the 125 kHz lasers, how they bounce back to the computer onboard the plane, what's involved in translating with the algorithms, rendering, dot clouds, etc. will wait for another day.

•

So, May Day, 2012 was a promising and good day – everything worked as planned, and there was some keeper-video recorded. Onward to tomorrow, the first day of the rest of our lives and a leading indicator of what's in store for us.

"I'm on the bus," pilot Charles Gross III assured us when the session in Command HQ ended at 2200 hours.

•

It became clearer to me today that this whole project is about documenting - recording images on several levels. We're documenting the process and story on video, with emphasis on how this LiDAR can help tell the history of civilization with digital imagery. Then there's a fair amount of documenting the documentation and the documenters. When we have actual LiDAR imaging results, that documentation and its implications will be the prime focus. We are living with the built-in irony of using the most

state of the art laser and computer-rendering technology juxtaposed with the targets, which are remnants of ancient civilizations, likely 800-1,000 years old. That's a running theme.

Commander Elkins has set himself up as frequent on-camera commentator/explainer. Probably tomorrow several of us will go on-camera to tell what we think is about to happen and what we expect to find out, both on the first trip over **T1** in the morning, and for the next several days. We have a shared goal, but the vision of it probably varies from guy to guy. Those expectations, recorded before any LiDAR results, might be good juxtaposition for before and after editable material.

We spent many hours yesterday learning

#7 We Have Dot Clouds!

Wednesday, May 2, 2012
Roatan, Bay Islands, Honduras

The first day of flying was as good as anyone could have asked. Pilot Chuck and Juan Carlos, who is also a pilot and world-class LiDAR tech, took off about 7:30 from Roatan after a video session that recorded their attitudes and documented the plane itself.

So cramped! And sizzling hot inside according to the fliers and the shooter, Commander Elkins. And the air-conditioning system doesn't work—great for the tropics, huh?

Their mission, including a stop for fueling at the end, pushed the limits of our aerial and

technical capabilities. And they succeeded. They spent the entire scanning portion of the trip over target area 1 (**T1**), using a flight pattern and plan Juan had created. It was essentially oval—what he compared to the efficiency and methodology of a Zamboni pattern on a hockey rink.

Doug Preston compared it to the most efficient way to brush a clay tennis court so that there was overlap to be certain not to miss any portion, but doing it in a curvy way, rather than simply like the back and forth of mowing a lawn.

Chuck was pleased that they made 31 passes in the limited time available. As best I understand—and many here can correct me where I'm wrong—what's going on is that they fly less than 2,000 feet over the target area and in a coordinated synergy of technical elements start shooting millions of 125 kHz laser blasts of at wavelength of 1064 nanometers toward the ground. A very small percentage of beams is able to penetrate the dense jungle canopy— think of rays of sunlight when you're in a forest.

At locations where there is a clearing, a river or thinner brush, a much higher percentage of the beams gets through. When the beams hit something—tree tops, branches, brush, or the ground—they bounce back at the speed of light to the on-board computer system. The system registers the data and makes it possible to process and determine what, if anything, is there, how big it is, its topography, and how it looks when tilted various ways to determine its three-dimensionality. It can also determine the make-up of an object in terms of its density as well as some other stuff.

Long and short, when the data from the plane returns to the Parrot Tree on a hard drive, Michael and Abhinav will take it, transfer it to their laptop, filter that data with the GPS coordinate readouts from our spots—

here, Dulce de Nombre de Culmi and Trujillo— and compile all of it into a master file which is read by a complex set of programs that can interpret it. Then it takes some hours to graphically render the output so it is readable on a laptop. At that point, it can be viewed and manipulated in several permutations.

•

By 9 o'clock Wednesday evening, Michael was able to show us some of what the first day's mission had accomplished by selecting a small section of the target area and fiddling with the results.

Cautious as ever, Michael would make no big conclusions other than to say that it was all working – meaning that he was judging that there was enough data in that limited sample

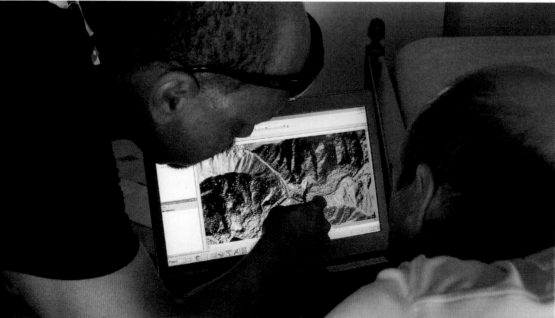

to be able to study and analyze it to determine what was down there and how it looked. Making actual conclusions and analyzing the data takes a whole lot more time and experimentation than just a first-blush test.

But as we looked at the rendered data we do have "plenty of dot clouds," according to our interpreters. With ample dot clouds we will be able to manipulate the data to find out lots of what we came here to do. All of this is scientifically amazing, even to totally untrained eyes like mine.

•

On the documentation front, we screened footage from the last two days and did some critical thinking and talking about the priorities for our visual storytelling—seeing the whole picture for run and shoot verité situations and understanding that what's on the video is all that the audience is ever going to see. The goal is to make sure that the footage is solid, shows what's going on, but isn't wasteful of the editor and production team's time—i.e., think about sequences, don't leave the camera rolling when you know nothing's happening or you're setting up the next shot, and always be aware of the audio so that when people are talking it'll be right or else it's useless. (BTW, my own tendency has usually leaned toward shooting more to get spontaneous moments, rather than being cautious.)

Steve Graham, Mark, and Roberto spent much of the afternoon shooting environmental (art and beauty) shots of our lovely surroundings and the crew doing what they do. In the evening, we did set-up interviews with Juan and Chuck debriefing their first day. All real good, usable documentation. Very interesting commentary about the process of flying and scanning, what they saw and eye-balled—which corroborated much of our earlier expectations about **T1**—and their interaction as a team came through clearly. Both Chuck and Juan reported seeing white splotches from the air. It's still a mystery, but our guys are working on discovering that and more.

•

Flying Day 2 starts at 7 AM. We're hoping the uncontrollables—weather and tech—hold up so it can be as productive as Day 1.

Tomorrow and Friday the entire valley of **T1** will be scanned, crisscrossed and overlapped, assuming the weather and technical operations continue to be as favorable as they were on this maiden voyage.

This afternoon, when Bill Bennenson arrived, four of the Honduran National Guardsmen staged this mock arrest for a photo op. Bill seemed to enjoy it.

#8 Hair Balls R Us
Friday, May 4, 2012
Roatan, Bay Islands, Honduras

From the start of this project, we have been besieged with one challenge after another.

Today was no exception. The most difficult and troubling came after a successful scanning mission over **T1** and part of **T2**. After more than two hours of covering more than 20 lines, Chuck landed the Cessna in La Ceiba to refuel, just as he had done for the last two days.

Today they were pushing the envelope. They arrived with about 20 gallons of aviation fuel in the tank—not much, and certainly nowhere near enough to get back to Roatan.

When they went to refuel, they were told that there was no fuel at the airport. We had chosen La Ceiba, the third largest city in Honduras, as the refueling location because it was the closest place to get aviation gas—an extremely tightly controlled substance in these days of cracking down on the planes of the narcotics transporters. La Ceiba was to be our place to get aviation gas for the duration of our mission. Bruce and Steve had set it up with the government agency for aviation and the other offices that issue permits for the scarce fuel. Of course, there is none in Roatan. Lots of jet fuel there for commercial airlines - but no aviation gas.

So there they were in midafternoon in La Ceiba. Bruce got on the phone from our Palapa Bar and Grill. We found out from Juan Carlos that they had no idea when the fuel might arrive. They had been told that it would be coming shortly.

With some cell phone shenanigans, Bruce managed to find out that the tank truck—a big one from San Pedro Sula—would be arriving around 5 or 5:30. Our guys could refuel and get "home" to Roatan for dinner.

Everyone was worried about getting the data from today's scanning back to Mike at rendering central—his room at Parrot Tree. It was decided that Doug Preston, who had been cramped in the back of the Cessna—all 6'3" of him without a seat for some six hours—would take the data on a hard drive on a commercial flight departing around 4 and arriving in Roatan before 5pm.

The aviation gas was supposed to arrive around 5-5:30 PM. But as we know, this is Honduras where what can go wrong all too frequently does. The big truck with the fuel

had a tire blowout on the road between San Pedro Sula and La Ceiba. Now nobody knew when it would arrive.

Chuck and Juan and the plane with all the expensive equipment on it seemed to be stuck in La Ceiba. Now what? They could sleep in a hotel there, but the plane with its top-secret hardware must be secured at all times—that's why we're paying to keep that group of Honduran national soldiers on duty 24/7. Of course, Captain Garcia and his men were back in Roatan waiting. One solution—go to the Honduran/DEA Air Force Base in La Ceiba, show them the papers, maybe get Bruce to call

them or their bosses, and get them to stand guard for the night while our guys stay in La Ceiba.

At this writing, I'm not sure what happened, except that Juan and Chuck wound up back in Roatan for a very late dinner. The only way to get here was to fly. I'm not sure if they got fuel and returned, albeit a few hours late, or if they got a commercial flight and left the plane. Or, if they got a charter, maybe it was from the same pilot/company we contracted with on Sunday to fly from Roatan to San Pedro and back with the helicopter to plant the GPS units. Tune in tomorrow for that answer.

In a video debrief, Doug compellingly told how magnificent the jungle was—all that amazing rich green with some purple vegetation with flowers at the top of many, and the breathtaking beauty of the entire valley, apparently untouched by humans for a real long time. "There we were, at about 2,000 feet, using the most modern technology to shoot millions of harmless laser beams into this thick and impenetrable jungle that human beings might not have been in for maybe 1,000 years." His observations were concrete. His sensibility that we were really onto a discovery was overpowering. "To be part of this whole project is an honor," beamed a tired but now-confirmed Lost Boy, Douglas Preston.

•

Back at the Parrot Tree, the (local) worker bees stayed busy with various kinds of image making. Michael is the point person in data

Meanwhile, Doug Preston, world-class author and adventurer, bought the $37 ticket and made the flight back to Roatan. Doug delivered the goods—the LiDAR digital data along with telephoto still images and wide-angle video of the jungle and the interior of the plane. What a champ!

They are all unique elements and I am just about positive they will be part of our documentary. His shooting was remarkably steady as he stretched his long arms out to get the images. Only once did his cramped outstretched legs accidentally bump against the LiDAR equipment and hit the switch to turn it off. Fortunately, that incident caused only a minor 360 turn by Chuck to restart the line he had been scanning before the turn-off. Doug was a trooper! And the images he brought were stupendous. He was exuberant when he got back to the resort. We were too.

screening. With the additional input of Thursday's impressive data (some 41 rows) he's able to put together full views of the majority of the **T1** site—aka "Elkins Valley" or can we still call it "**Sukia Tara**?"

While always prefacing his observations with "I'm not an archaeologist, but..." Mike did see some formations and possible locations that he said could not be explained as natural phenomena. What they were and are, of course, we don't know yet. And despite our tendency to get immediate gratification as 21st-century electronic explorers with a let's-figure-it-out-now mentality, most likely, it will take many moons to effectively manipulate the data in and draw any exciting (and perhaps historical) conclusions.

Everyone here, including Bill, Steve, Bruce and I, as well as those who aren't here like Virgilio and reportedly Africo Madrid and President Lobo, want answers ASAP. But, we do understand that the gathering of the data is a well-defined science, while the interpretation and puzzling it out to determine the whereabouts of the stuff we are after is a whole lot more like a craft or an art—one which Abhinav and Michael are our resident experts.

There are also a few of the NCALM team in Houston poring over the data with fresh and experienced eyes, but there was a mini-hairball about the transfer of data to them. Michael told me he wanted to do the transfer first thing this morning. Obviously, he wanted to talk it over with Steve to be sure he was cool with sending the images back to the senior members of the Houston team.

Michael did the right thing. A set of emails ensued. It got thorny along the way because Michael had used the word "permission" and saying that he was getting it from Steve in his

communications with Houston. The senior guys at University of Houston got a bit territorial about whose data it is—the client's (us) or the researchers' (them). It was finally resolved and as per our agreement, all the data would eventually be available and held by NCALM, but that would occur if and when we did what we wanted and needed to do with it.

With the morning hair ball taken care of, the guys in Houston are ready to get to it and do some analyzing. We shall see what they come up with. The technicians who are screening it have signed a non-disclosure statement, but Steve was concerned and didn't want to send any of "our proprietary results" to the sister operational group in Berkeley. He didn't know them personally and they had not signed any NDA. It's all fixed now and we can't wait to hear the reactions of all these scientific experts who have world-class knowledge and many years of looking at LiDAR data. Will the Lost City of the Mosquitia jungle be uncovered in Houston, Texas? It might sound trite, but, we live in such an intertwined global digital world that anything's possible.

•

Roberto Ysais continued to shoot, shoot, shoot and now has more than 1,000 pictures of our process, results, and people. Someone remarked that if we're here another week, Roberto will know all there is to know about the island and its people. He did score a nice restaurant about a mile up the road in the direction nobody had been. **Cal's Temporary Cantina** was a delightful change from the hotel's Palapa Grill & Bar—both the food and the ambiance.

Bill and Steve picked up the tab. UTL has been consistently generous and has provided

us with the best creature comforts and professional capabilities possible all along.

Steve and Mark shot an interview with **Lindell Bodden**, the GM of the Parrot Tree about her multinational roots in the Bay Islands and the island of Manhattan. She provided some fascinating perspective on her family history, including talking about her 104-year-old uncle who lives in **Puerto Lempira** and spent his whole life in the Mosquitia. What an interview he would be—a unique take on the history of the Mosquitia and the legend of Ciudad Blanca. We're hoping to see him here on Monday, but is a 104-year-old gonna fly here?

Over the past 24 hours or so we also shot a series of sit-down interviews with the different team members. Here's a quick summary:

Steve Elkins ran down the background history of the project, from our attempts in the mid 90's until now. He explained why we're here and what we're doing.

Michael Sartori explained the process of how the LiDAR works and his sense of what we're doing and how it's going so far from his perspective as senior in loco tech.

Doug Preston articulated his fascinating description as a star reporter/philosopher of the scope and significance of this project.

Abhinav Singhania talked about what he does as the manipulator of the LiDAR data and a member of the team. He thinks of his role as a jack-of-all-trades in the technology.

Roberto Ysais told about the dichotomy between being in front of and behind the camera. He philosophized about documentation and art

Tom Weinberg - Doug Preston got me to tell the history of my long-term involvement with the search for the Lost City and how I felt about establishing a legacy as a successful discoverer. I found myself articulating

previously unexpressed personal feelings including how I wasn't trying to get famous. In fact, I knew enough about it to spurn it.

•

Meanwhile, **Bruce Heinicke** sat by the bar and told stories on-camera to Steve Elkins and me about his and Mabel's process of making this project happen with the blessing of Honduran officials and (parts of) the underlying reasons they want us to succeed. The video interview segued into real process when Bruce answered the cell phone and barked – in English and Spanish as only he can do it.

•

Saturday should be a day just like any other. Figuring out and solving the fuel situation, scanning more of **T2** and maybe some of **T3**—Michael's Kentucky Derby pick to be the big winner—are at the top of the agenda.

As usual, please tune in tomorrow for the events and hair balls. Just like at Churchill Downs, past performances probably won't be an indicator of the future.

#9 Cinco de Mayo
Saturday May 5, 2012
Roatan, Bay Islands, Honduras

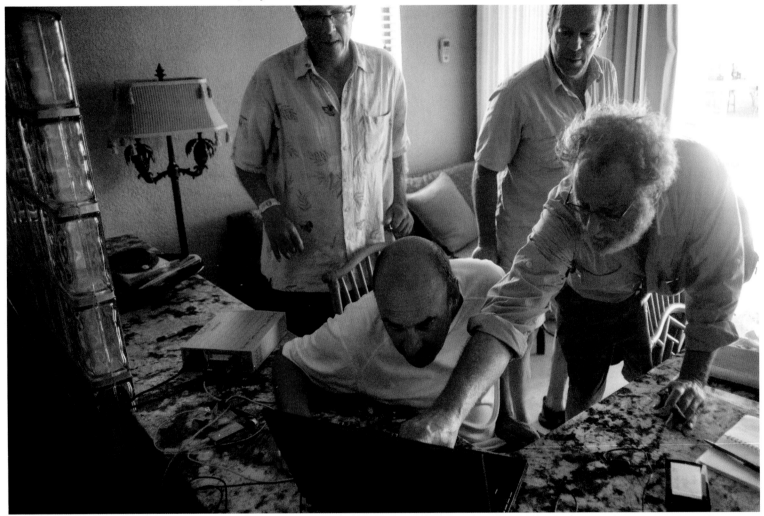

Holy shit!

Mild-mannered LiDAR senior technician Mike Sartori spends about 11 hours a day, eyes peeled to the laptop computer in his room. Each time he sees something he finds interesting or unusual, he notes it in his 6-inch spiral notebook. It's filled with coordinates and descriptions of features revealed by the LiDAR-generated data.

At about 11:40 this morning, when he was

Doug pointed out the straight lines on the LiDAR rendering, "There are no straight lines like these in nature."

looking at a readout of images from **T1**—**"Elkins Valley"**—he saw a set of images that he had never seen before. He recorded the coordinates and wrote "Holy Shit!" under them - totally out of character for the cautious, meticulous, sometimes skeptical Mike. The tipoff to look there came from a jpeg sent by **Bill Carter,** the granddaddy of LiDAR in the States and the founder of NCALM, who told Mike to explore that area further. It paid off.

His "Holy Shit" is like the Holy Grail for us Lost Boys.

Mike is a cautious soul. He's unlikely to say much of anything that might morph him from technical supervisor into a subjective analyst. But this time he just couldn't help himself. Mike saw and demonstrated to Steve and Bill and the rest of us a location that featured what could only be the indicators of a human civilization tucked into a protected area of **T1.**

What the LiDAR showed were unmistakable images of a set of structures buried in the jungle, public buildings and carved out spaces that almost undeniably appeared to be a complex and large, maybe a quarter mile-long group of what must be considered untouched human settlements. Hardly a chance in a zillion that all of these were naturally-occurring land features.

Our speculation ranged from it being a true lost city—whether or not it is the **"Ciudad Blanca"**—and its role as the center of a culture perhaps unknown for hundreds of years and possibly not Mayan or Toltec or other known civilizations. Were these stubs of structures public buildings, a possible temple, and was it a ball court-type open space all situated in a location that appeared to use the natural topography logically for security—defensive positions—and access—ways to get in and out by water and over land?

As with all these findings, the only way to

know for certain is to go there—but at least now we know exactly where we want to go.

•

Steve Graham and Mark shot an interview with Mike and verité footage of Abhinav at the laptop, explaining what we were looking at to Steve, Bill, Doug and me. I don't think anyone in the room doubted the validity of the images on the screen or the widespread potential implications of this preliminary indication of human habitat in the middle of a previously unexplored jungle.

We talked about it for hours, starting with shots and discussion recorded on video inside Mike's room, beginning with a "Hey, come look at this"—with the only Take 2 of the shooting that I know of—and extending to a walking interview with Doug and Steve on the far beach around 12:30.

That was followed by an interview I did with Bill, set in a jungle-like spot, about how the day's discoveries changed the entire flow of this project and maybe history.

OMG! We had actually located The Lost City of the Mosquitia—or at least A Lost City.

The fever was contagious. Handshakes, big smiles of near-euphoria, and bubbling-over gushing emanated from Room #403, right next to the Commander's.

Elkins was thrilled that "a bunch of PhD's in Houston had come to the same conclusions" and corroborated our findings out here "in the field." Whatever it was that we had uncovered, it was backed up by the experienced eyes of NCALM senior LiDAR management, **Ramesh Shrestha** in Houston and **Bill Carter** who was screening the low-rez data at his vacation

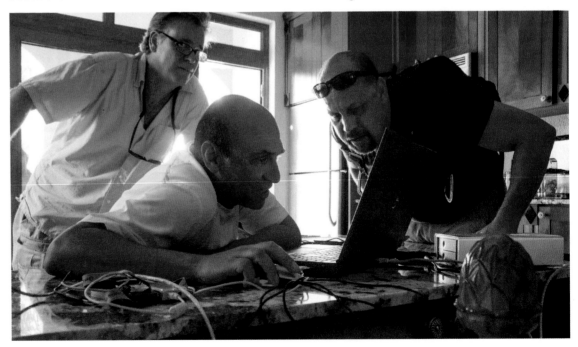

home in West Virginia and wanted more detailed data to study. It's not easy to get that much information sent via email in an effective way. Michael said he wouldn't be surprised if Ramesh, his boss and the director, might come here to be present at the creation and pick up goody-points for NCALM.

When Bruce resurfaced around 1 o'clock, and heard the current state of discovery, he wanted to get Africo Madrid and maybe President Pepe Lobo on the phone to invite them over to be part of the official video documentation of the discovery by LiDAR of the location of the Lost City, Ciudad Blanca, **City of the Monkey God**. If the Prez comes, so will Bruce's wife Mabel from St. Louis. Actually, she might come tomorrow anyhow—Bruce has been on his own for nearly two weeks and he needs support beyond what I and others have been able to supply.

Will Lobo come? TV cameras are powerful weapons of mass communication and he has a story to tell about Honduras. Just today, he cut the ribbon on the Maya 2012 Exhibit at University of Pennsylvania museum in Philadelphia. Virgilio and the IHAH might be on a roll. Don't rule out the possibility of seeing Lobo and/or Africo Madrid here at the Parrot Tree Resort in the coming days, shaking hands and heralding the archaeological breakthrough in Honduras using 21st-century technology to see through the jungle canopy and find human settlements never before known. He might assert that his country will be examining its rich cultural heritage as thoroughly and responsibly as possible—high-falutin language that incorporates the threat that anyone who messes with it will be treated in a manner they deserve.

Where we go from here was addressed cogently by Bill in his 45-minute interview with me. In his roles as executive producer and true friend of the earth, his perspective rang true— "We are in an entirely different position with this project than we were 24 hours ago."

Bill's big-picture consciousness about the importance of our documentation work to influence intelligent handling of the ecological and physical resources moving forward is of critical importance. He realizes that in order to make that happen responsibly it means that the Honduran government will have to take all steps required. But, Bill also emphasizes that once the word is out on our discovery – and it must be handled as wisely as possible – it will require partners with resources (money) to assure that it proceeds and evolves in the most protective way and with long-term awareness built in to every step of the journey of discovery.

OK, what have we done so far?

• We've determined that it is almost certain something non-natural exists in this curious valley.

• We've shown the effectiveness of LiDAR to get accurate readings of the surface below the thickest jungle canopy.

• We've changed the paradigm for the nature of discovery (at least preliminary identification) of remote places that nobody has ever been or explored.

• We've documented our process every step of the way using state-of-the-art video, audio and still photography.

• We've worked as a remarkably in-sync unit with 12 specialists dedicating their considerable skills to a single goal. It would never have happened without all the links in the Elkins-Captain Morgan chain, dating back more than 17 years.

So – **Cinco de Mayo, 2012**! A day that might well be recognized as the dawning of the age of successful **Joystick Discovery**.

53

#10 LiDAR Interruptus
Sunday, May 6, 2012
Roatan, Bay Islands, Honduras

Juan Carlos and Chuck Gross got to the airport at the usual time around 7 AM. During the first few minutes in the air on the way to fuel up in La Ceiba, Juan wasn't able to get the LiDAR box to turn on.

Back on the ground, he had no success either. The LiDAR was dead—an electronic glitch that occurs once every year or so, shutting down our mission for an undetermined period of time.

Chuck and Juan called back to HQ and returned by 9. Michael and Juan tried to figure it out, but they are not open-the-black-box guys. They are software technicians and airborne surveyors—and damn good ones. Meanwhile, the tech maintenance team working under contract with Houston NCALM is in **Toronto, Ontario**, and on Sundays they have only one support guy on duty. Their associates and bosses won't be in until Monday morning.

There seem to be three possible outcomes:

• On the phone with Juan, Michael and Abhinav, the techs can talk and walk them through a basic plug-unplug sequence to wake up the LiDAR box. Unlikely—but a wonderful possible outcome.

• A tech will have to fly from Canada to Roatan with parts and tools. This has many implications. Timing, of course, is the critical path. We can't afford to sit here very long without flying the remaining missions over some designated parts of **T1**, then **T2** and **T3**—something on the order of three to four days of additional flying. If that can't start for another 4 or 5 days we've got real problems.

• Lastly, we abort or at least lighten the overhead here and do the best we can to complete our scanning later in the week.

Late in the afternoon, we recorded "a panel show" with Steve, Juan, Michael and Abhinav. Ten of us were in the room. They went through their experiences with and understanding of downed LiDAR. Michael said it could be at least three down days and likely more.

Bill spoke of the options, reassuring us that, if at all possible, the mission must go on so we can get all the data we came for. Doug clearly expressed his sense that this is the only time we'll ever have this team together to do the mission. Onward!

Steve brought up the possibility of getting a helicopter from the government and checking out our identified human settlement sites—perhaps even trying to land close enough to actually eyeball and touch the ground-reality.

And all of this is intertwined with the political complications and intrigue we now understand from Mabel's conversation with Africo Madrid.

Africo says he wants—or is it plans?—to be here on Wednesday. His big picture agenda is to see what we have. And then, if he believes that what we have uncovered is unquestionable —and he "trusts us 100%," says Mabel—he will tell his boss, President Lobo, and the head of Congress, **Juan Orlando Hernandez**, to come over on Thursday.

As I get it, Africo will be accompanied by **Francisco Bueso**, the budget and money official for the government.

The in-and-out political and personal sagas of Virgilio Paredes continue to be a juicy subplot of the larger story. It sure seems as if, at the very least, he's fallen from grace—even of his lifelong and family friend and political patron, Carlos Africo Madrid. Vigilio is scheduled to arrive in Roatan on Tuesday. We are now under strict instructions to show him nothing. Nada.

All of this technical and political maneuvering plays into the financial realities of UTL and our expedition. The positioning and timing of any announcements vis-a-vis our partner must be coordinated properly. We do not want the government to preempt us or say the wrong thing. Nor do we want to misrepresent what we have – preliminary and indicative data of discovery, but not a sure-thing ground truth. The miracle is that we know even this much after a few days of shooting laser beams into the jungle. More results will be coming in over the days, weeks and months ahead.

So, the first task is for **Garry Spire** and me to write some guidelines for a press release so we can be ready if we need it quickly for both us and the government to use. Their timing seems complicated by the need to pass a new law in the legislature in order for Africo, Lobo, Orlando Hernandez and company to be rock-solid on their ability to protect the areas that we have designated as likely archaeological sites. This is a legal/political challenge, but probably must be taken care of pronto.

As with all matters Honduran, money, land, power, and influence must all must be dealt with simultaneously. And it's hard to get a straight read when the stories are changing almost constantly. But like the good boy scout discoverers we are trying to be, we need to **Be Prepared**.

There's no upside for us at this point to hype our truth until we know for sure what's really out there. To keep the government on the same page is critical. In fact, the story of what we have is not a product. It's proof that it can be done – i.e., we found almost certain indicators of human life in a place where nobody has known it existed. We have changed the way stuff is found. We have seen how this technology can be used to map, chart, define, and identify what's under the jungle canopy in places where it is virtually impossible to go to by land.

So, this is not just an archeological hunt for some lost city. It is also a way—for the first time ever—to see the geology, rain forest plants and the relief structure of a region. This has implications for a multitude of other places and applications worldwide. Not sure who, but someone called this project "the poster child of conserving natural habitats like this isolated rain forest."

At a 9 o'clock Palapa pow-wow, Bruce's wife **Mabel**, who arrived today, ran down the internal Hondo politics based on her talks with Africo. Bill wanted to establish that what we're doing is 100% legal and is with the cooperation and involvement of the Honduran government.

What we have now may not be a simply defined or conventional "discovery." But taken together, our satellite photos, the still photographs and video from above and the LiDAR digital data rendered into 3-D imagery make a great case. However, the Honduran government—and eventually the rest of the world—as Bill says, "must accept the cyber-truth of our May 5, 2012 initial discovery."

#11 The Pilot Can Swim
Monday, May 7, 2012
Roatan, Bay Islands, Honduras

Chuck Gross didn't need to fly with the LiDAR today. He spent most of the day in the lagoon —somebody gossiped that he looked like a hippopotamus. I'm sure he enjoyed himself, but would not have appreciated the description!

The LiDAR also remained on the ground for a day of rest. Steve, Bruce, and Bill doggedly pursued the ways and means for the technician to get here as soon as possible from Canada, where **Optech**, the manufacturer of the LiDAR,

claims they that are the biggest in the world.

The company says: *"Optech is the world's leading maker of reliable, rugged, and innovative LiDAR survey products, with over 35 years of experience worldwide."*

They manufacture lots of products. The one we're using and that needs fixing or replacing ASAP is **ALTM Gemini** airborne laser terrain mapper for wide-area mapping.

8 AM Update

With the box officially in need of a house call, the technician is being dispatched from Toronto, and it's not like falling off a log. He'll have to get customs clearance first to get into the US, and again once he gets here to Roatan. We most fervently hope that he will bring the replacement parts he needs to get us up and flying by Wednesday morning. That would mean we'd have had no-fly for three days, Sunday, Monday and Tuesday. In fact, there is a small chance that we could do a few rows on Tuesday afternoon depending on when he's able to arrive, begins work and that he succeeds quickly.

•

On the documentary front, Bill and Doug did a long and informative interview/talk session in a jungly setting with two cameras and two mics. Good info for use in the doc, no doubt, but it's

also good to articulate our understanding about what we are doing, have done, how to deal with the government about it, how to characterize and position our successes and how to let the rest of the world know what we've done.

At dusk, Steve and Mark shot a half hour+ with Mabel on her porch, telling Doug the whole story of the first time she latched on to then President-elect, Porfirio "Pepe" Lobo, at a church in Tegoose. The way she told it—sometimes telling of a three-minute occurrence in 15 minutes—it's clear that she and Bruce gave credit to divine intervention following the death of her father.

Whatever way it can be explained, the contact was made, Lobo made a commitment,

spoke to Bruce on the phone in St. Louis, and Lobo's #1 man, Africo Madrid, was told right outside the church to do absolutely everything possible to make our expedition a success.

That was over two years ago. And even with dozens of bureaucratic and logistical hair balls between then and now, here we are, we have found some real things, and Africo remains our best ally.

In fact, Africo Madrid plans to be here on Wednesday with his mother **Carole Hart** from Florida and the finance minister and to see what we have and talk through the next steps. Assuming all is kosher, President Lobo and the head of Congress, Juan Orlando Hernandez, are supposed to be here in Roatan on Thursday.

We have prepared a new draft of guidelines

for initial press release. This is the updated press draft (v3.2) which was drafted by Garry and me and shown around on May 8, 2012:

UTL Press Release v.3.2

As of May __ , 2012.

UTL Explorations, LLC, today announced the completion of the first-ever airborne LiDAR imaging survey of previously-uncharted areas of the Mosquitia jungle, undertaken with the full cooperation of the Government of Honduras.

The privately-funded survey utilized an advanced $1.5 million dual-laser scanning system to peer below dense rainforest canopy, to reveal what preliminary data indicates is new and convincing archaeological evidence of human settlement patterns located in areas of the Mosquitia that have been historically associated with legends surrounding the purported existence of a lost ancient civilization variously known through the past five centuries as Ciudad Blanca or the White City.

The cutting-edge survey marks the first application of airborne-sensing LiDAR technology to reveal and chart what lies beneath this area's previously impenetrable mountainous rainforest canopy.

First indications of human settlement patterns, possibly on a large scale, will continue to be analyzed in greater depth by digital imagery specialists, archaeologists, and other experts on the project team based in Honduras and the United States.

The digital data acquired during the survey bring enormous potential benefits to the people of Honduras in the form of improved conservation, rain-forest and watershed resource management, along with first-ever surface-mapping of areas lying below the canopy which has never before been comprehensively charted or fully explored in modern times.

The project was undertaken by UTL Expeditions with the full cooperation and support of the Government of Honduras, its Instituto de Antropologia y Historia (IHAH), and in conjunction with the National Center for Airborne Laser Mapping (NCALM), affiliated with the University of Houston and University of California Berkeley, USA.

Further research of the imaging and results will continue for several months by NCALM, in association with archaeological and cultural experts. UTL has documented the process of this scientific breakthrough on digital video.

•

This is subject to changes as we see fit, but it is a starting point so that we don't get caught without our own set of words. (I also see it as the template for what we will work out as a joint statement with the Honduran government, but we shall see.)

Tune in tomorrow. The LiDAR will be fixed—we hope—and we will "do the fix" with Virgilio after he arrives.

#12 The Tool Box!?!
Tuesday, May 8, 2012
Roatan, Bay Islands, Honduras

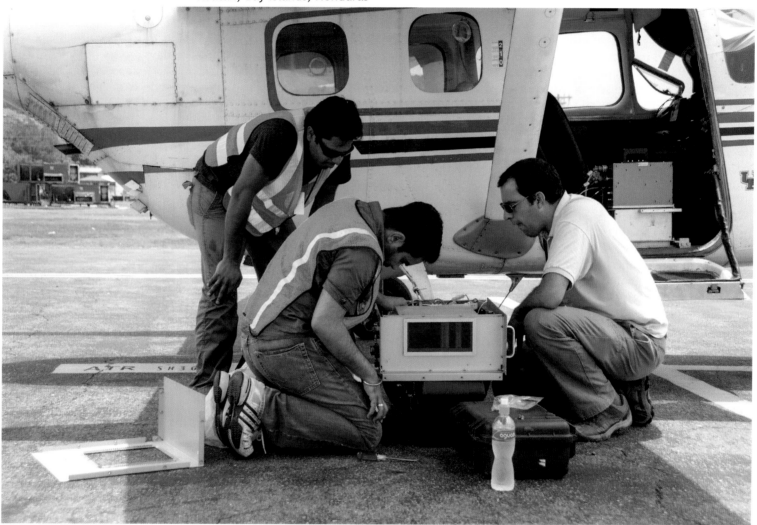

Mehta Yogeshwar Varun, the Fixer of LiDAR from Optech in Toronto arrived in Roatan – amazingly less than 24 hours after he was dispatched by his company with pressure from NCALM and Commander Elkins.

Mehta flew Toronto - DC, DC - San Salvador, San Salvador - Roatan. Steve picked him up about 10:30 AM and then spent the rest of the day on the phone and online tracking down what happened to Mehta's two bags. He

61

couldn't work without his tools.

His bags had checked through US Customs as they left Canada and they did arrive via **United Airlines** at Dulles in Washington last night. They were checked all the way through to Roatan on the baggage checks—but they were never transferred to **Avianca/Taca** for the last two legs of the trip. I'm not sure if Mehta was required to do that himself or whether they were supposed to be moved directly from United to Taca by the baggage handlers. But I am sure that he should have had a name tag on the duffel bag with the tools. The other bag, a hard case, did have contact information. I assume he's a good LiDAR tech, but I'm also sure his social and travel tech could be better.

Bill's travel agents in Los Angeles tried and tried with Taca and United. Finally, my local hero, **Lomar Martinez** —our young transport fixer—found out through his pals at Taca at the Roatan airport that the bags were still in Washington. They arranged to have the bags sent to San Salvador on the afternoon plane, but they won't get in here to Roatan until the afternoon plane from SAL arriving about 4 PM tomorrow.

At dinner at Cal's (real good snapper), the 13 members of our group gave a heartfelt toast, "To the tool box!" (Actually, there was a Take 2 for Roberto's photo.) Virgilio was there. He enjoys a good meal—especially his favorite kind (free). Bruce and Mabel did not eat with us. Bruce was driving home from the airport earlier in the day and had to pull over because his vision was impaired for a few minutes. They made it back and he mostly stayed in the room for many hours, stressed with high blood pressure. Bruce is in terrible shape, let's face it. Sixty-four and looking many years older. Trouble moving, walking, breathing. He still

smokes about three packs a day, wheezing and using the inhaler and taking heart medicine every night. Let's just hope his strength, fostered by his life-long history of "Doing What You Have to Do to Get the Job Done," continues for a good long while—but, ya never know.

Excellent video interview with Captain Chuck Gross conducted by Doug with additional input from Bill and Garry. Commander Elkins shot at

the airport as Mehta arrived empty-handed. Not sure what else was shot.

Dare we call the missing parts and tools another layer of hair ball or just fate or was he just a bit naïve or careless? Whatever the proximate cause, UTL Expeditions, LLC and its

subsidiary UTL Adventures, have been paying for a cast of more than a dozen for a total of 11 nights now—from Saturday, April 28 through today, May 8—and we have only been able to fly for four days. Each LiDAR scan over the jungle is less than three hours. The remainder of the days are spent flying to and from Roatan, with fuel stops in La Ceiba. And the rest of their time is mainly resort living—eating, drinking, swimming, reading, on computer and phone. Plus a bit of project planning.

Total time scanning the targets on this project so far—10-12 hours. No-fly for first three days, fly four days, no-fly for the next four—that's assuming no scanning tomorrow. If we get the plane back over the jungle on

Thursday with the LiDAR functioning properly and good weather, it's possible to go back to our area of most interest in **T1** and then do some lines in **T3**. Then on Friday we'll finish **T3** and on Saturday try to do some or all of **T4**. Saturday night will mark two weeks to the day after the arrival of the gang of 12 – and my 16th day in Roatan.

Sounds like an over-run on the 7-10 days we had thought it would be. But the amazing and wonderful thing is that we keep finding more impressive evidence of human settlements under the canopy. Michael and Abhinav have stayed on the box doing their art and science to find stuff. And tonight, a colorized image from their boss, Ramesh in Houston, looks very, very interesting.

•

Tune in tomorrow and on Thursday when Africo arrives, his mother Carole and, supposedly, the finance minister in tow. He told Mabel on phone that he had a big session with Virgilio Paredes yesterday. Virgilio confirmed that meeting. I suspect that they have quite different versions of what was said. My best guess is that Virgilio got the riot act read to him, likely including some threatening rhetoric. But, the true balance of power in Honduran politics is virtually impossible to know.

#13 Taking Flight
Wednesday Night, May 9, 2012
Roatan, Bay Islands, Honduras

The LiDAR is fixed! If the weather, the plane, and the technology stay friendly we'll have three more days of scanning – Thursday, Friday and Saturday.

We want to find out some things about **T3** since we haven't been there yet.

We want to go back and get higher resolution scans of our identified sites in **T1** as requested by LiDAR NCALM maven Bill Carter in Houston.

Bill Benenson cautions that we ought to

proceed as if every flight is the last one. That means go to **T3** first on Thursday, do a couple shots at **T1** toward the end of the day and see where we get after that. We just might have some new and remarkable info by tomorrow night.

Africo arrives on Friday, with his mother Carole and the minister of finance. Possibly with his wife also—not sure about kids. Africo wants to host the first and probably the only LiDAR Fiesta on Sabado to take everyone to dinner, including the mayor of Roatan, the Bay Islands governor, and whoever else. He told Mabel that none of us should make any other plans. Everybody loves a Saturday night.

Vigilio was omnipresent today. Confab with Bill, Steve and Garry at the breakfast table about the importance of a joint press release and having the same story. We later discussed it in Steve's room. Virgilio is one-tracked about needing to touch the ruins, to be able to tell people that there is tangible proof that it's real. And Virgilio wants to be the one to touch it. He thinks it'll be easy to go there in a military chopper next week and have some proof on the ground. He thinks big – but, of course he doesn't actually know where it is and NOBODY knows for sure where or if a helicopter can land there. Those are just minor details for Virgilio, perhaps the most lost of the Lost Boys.

Virgilio and Steve went to the sports bar for lunch and then to airport to pick up the two bags from the Taca flight. Virgilio is a man of many words who says that this country is ultimately a drug-dominated economy, that the government must cooperate, that the USA and DEA are in charge of much of military and civilian authority and that he sees no way that will change in the near future.

Heavy stuff.

When they got to the airport, Virgilio turned out to be a great asset. He flashed the Presidential card and Taca yes-sirred him, found the two bags immediately and turned them over. Off Steve and Virgilio went. No questions, no customs, no problems.

When there was a routine military road block on the way back to Parrot Tree, the soldiers ogled the box and bag in back of SUV. Apparently, when they saw the Presidential card they said all was fine and sent them on their way.

Virgilio can be helpful. Nobody knows how much he can be totally trusted, but we can and will work with him for the duration, however long that is. He ate dinner and talked for a couple hours with Bill and Garry. Doug and I were in on some of that as well. Virgilio has his agendas. We will have to pick and choose which of them we can accept and which are valid. Africo Madrid tells Virgilio what to do and when. So I assume nothing substantial will be decided without Sr. Africo. But, Virgilio is fun and cordial in any situation.

Our interview day started with Juan down by the sea at 6 AM. He was articulate and credible on the process, and revealed his personal passions about Honduras, Ciudad Blanca, old-time mapmaking and the place of LiDAR in the continuum of information about his country.

Juan Carlos Fernandez: "We will be the first to have a map of this area (the Mosquitia jungle) with an amazing amount of detail."

Juan is 95% convinced we have uncovered

with Virgilio at sunset. He appears to be much better than he was. Mabel might not agree completely—she gets the brunt of his crankiness.

And for the record, once the bags with parts and tools arrived it took Mehta from Optech just an hour or two to fix the navigation system. Before dinner, he and Juan screwed it into the plane at the airport so it would all be ready to fly in the morning.

Tomorrow we'll probably do a shoot with Steve, reviewing where we are with whole project. Friday will be Africo day. Saturday, too. And we'll likely leave for USA on Sunday. Of course, if all goes well, we'll also generate millions of dot clouds in the next three days – and we might even discover more stuff.

•

man-made signatures, "but this is just a first step in a long process. We now know where a needle is in the haystack. And of course we must go in and find it. We have no idea how old it is. The next step is to go in a helicopter and rappel..." Ah – 21st-century discovery. It all sounds so easy. Ha!

Juan's video interview by Steve, along with a few questions from me, is a classic for the archives. A few bites will definitely work in our documentary, but the full 40 minutes provides a terrific glimpse at the state-of-the-art, where LiDAR exploring fits in, how it matters in Honduras, the obstacles that have to be overcome, and how it takes a skilled team to make it all happen. It's a wonderful piece to archive for the ages.

Bruce was a no-show for breakfast and most of the day, but he did surface for a cocktail

#14 We Make History And We Learn From It
Thursday night, May 10, 2012
Roatan, Bay Islands, Honduras

Today's chronicle was not circulated in Roatan due to Garry's concern about what would happen "if it got into the wrong hands."

Bravo—the LiDAR flew today! In fact, it might have been the longest day of actual flying time. In totally clear weather—again, thankfully—

the LiDAR fly-boys, Chuck and Juan made more than 40 passes, starting with **T3** and going back for some hi-rez passes at our **T1** proven spot—aka "Sukia Tara." We'll know results in the morning, but on first glance and before full rendering, Michael was very encouraged about **T3**. He likes **T3** as a primo location for structures and habitation.

Chuck, fresh from flying over it, said, "If I were an Indian, that's where I'd live." I asked him what he meant and he explained that it seemed like a spot that was friendly in altitude, forestation, openings, etc. Plus, the river system is excellent. And, he thinks it's connected to **T1**, some 25 miles away as the crow flies. Who knows?

We will—someday.

Virgilio Paredes did an interview with Doug at dusk across the lagoon. There was a bit of a crowd interested in what he was saying – Bill, Garry and me, Commander Elkins shooting and Roberto taking stills pictures. It was about 30 minutes, some in Spanish but mostly in English.

Some of the highlights as best I could hear were:
• A rundown of the history of the legend and searches for Ciudad Blanca
• How Virgilio always knew we would find it using the high-tech satellites and LiDAR.
• How we (IHAH, the Honduran Government, UTL and our group) are all part of the same team, smoothly functioning like a watch to make it work.

• And how we definitely have succeeded and started a new way of doing archaeological, scientific, geologic mapping, and other scientific research. He said lots of other stuff – we'll have to screen the video. One thing he keeps saying is that we must get in there and see it—and he's eager to have it happen "on his watch."

Our evening task was to come up with a name for our spot in the valley of **T1**. Michael says it's a job for us—Bill, Steve, Doug and me. **Brad Elkins**, who flew in from Washington, D.C. this morning to see what his dad is doing, also participated in the naming process. Roberto, Mark, and others at Cal's (again) came up with the Spanish name for "awesome." I'm not

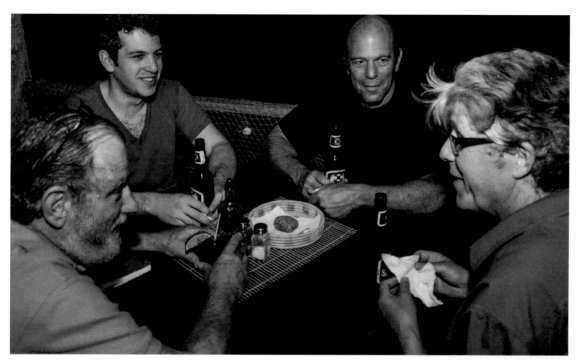

Honduras and Nicaragua. "Sukia" has been translated as "Medicine Man" referring to the colorful leader who conducted the ancient rituals. A fabled holy figure from these legends was known as "Dama Sukia Tara..."

Doug thought for a while and said he liked Sukia Tara, saying it was a name he thought Americans could relate to. Tune in tomorrow for that one, too. It might be nice to have a brand name for Africo Madrid when he arrives tomorrow afternoon with his wife, mother and the finance minister.

•

BTW, Bruce and Mabel went out to dinner with us. Bruce is looking lots better. He looked like the full-Bruce character with his small black straw stovepipe hat and night sunglasses.

sure what it was, but seemed kinda close to "macanudo" and we did not find a Jamaican cigar or an Argentinian comic strip.

Doug, Steve, Brad and I went through lots of possibilities and somehow returned to a term our group had made up for our brochure and proposal in 1996—**Sukia Tara**, then referred to as the **Lost City of the Monkey God**. It has genuine roots in the indigenous and Spanish heritage and is catchy enough for our backers and the public. At the time, as we were trying to raise funds for the expedition, we wrote:

What Is Sukia Tara? Many historians have interpreted the myths and legends of Sukia Tara —pronounced Sook'ya-Tara, sometimes written "Suk ya-Tara" and "Suk-ia Tara." The words come from the spoken language of the **Pech**, indigenous people who still live in the region that is part of the Mosquitia jungle of Eastern

#15 "The Most Explosive Film Project"
Thursday May 11, 2012
Roatan, Bay Islands, Honduras

Bill Benenson has been involved in plenty of films and projects. "This one," he said this morning, "is the most explosive I've ever been part of."

I see it as explosive on many levels:
• It's a breakthrough—what we've done has changed the world. Exploration will never be the same because of the way we applied LiDAR

to go places and find things that have never been seen. Our methodology sets a precedent for any similar future expeditions of discovery.

• The results we have achieved by finding definite signatures of human settlement beneath the canopy in this most dense and formidable jungle have major ramifications.

vast region. We have begun to piece together the possibilities for an integrated network of ancient settlements. (Archaeologists are careful with the word "civilizations.") We have identified structures and pinpointed several locations completely unknown until this project. Exploration of the places we have uncovered

Blanca has a life of its own and as Doug Preston says, "The White City legend, like most legends, probably has an important kernel of truth to it."

• Because it is impossible to control the coverage of events in our world of instantaneous communications, once this story is told, it likely will never stop bouncing—online, in print, and video. Never. We need to be as prepared as possible, knowing that the "news" will be reported and passed along in ways that we will never recognize as the truth we know.

This could become a prime example of what happens when media get ahold of a tale of the unknown. The one thing we know we have is primary video documentation of what we have been doing. And because Steve and I (and Bruce and Morgan) have been doggedly pursuing the history related to Ciudad Blanca for nearly 20 years, we have information, archival video and imagery that nobody else has or can have until we tell the story the way we want to tell it. That sounds like we're on to something explosive, right? But, it also has the potential to grab our tails and tales and spin them around the world.

• Sometimes it feels to me that the raw information we have in hand has a dynamic that is reminiscent of The Maltese Falcon. It has power beyond its intrinsic value. Maybe there is significant financial value that can come from our proprietary information. Could it lead to gold, relics, and gems—who knows? No doubt many people will think so and their greed and curiosity could lead to behavior that is, at the very least, unpredictable.

At this moment, only we—not even the Honduran government who has legal claim on everything discovered as cultural patrimony— know the exact locations of the settlements. That won't last for long. The Honduran officials, from the President on down, want to helicopter into the sites and see for themselves what's

Artist **Virgil Finlay**'s conceptional drawing of Theodore Modre's **"Lost City of the Monkey God."** Originally published in *The American Weekly*, September 22, 1940

People have searched the Mosquitia for hundreds of years in pursuit of Ciudad Blanca —The White City, sometimes known as the **Lost City of the Monkey God**. The legend has fascinated Hondurans and captivated people worldwide, and yet nobody has been able to do more than scratch the surface of this

this week will go on for decades, or maybe even centuries.

• This is an event that will capture the attention of the world - it is so remarkable. Even though we do not claim to have discovered the Lost City, we have found and located amazing stuff. The powerful legendary city of Ciudad

there. It could well happen within days or, more likely, many weeks. When that happens, what follows is likely to be, as Bill asserted, "muy explosive." Who documents that trip and how it is done are major considerations for our documentary and media gathering.

•

On the reality of our lives front, Friday was the fifth day of LiDAR scanning. Juan and Chuck had a full 3 hours of flying in the target areas. They started over a part of **T3** that we had thought to be a strong possible location for archaeological features. Then they went back and flew over parts of **T1**, thought to contain a pyramid or other feature from the LiDAR. **T1** has been dubbed **Ciudad Luna**, based on the fact that it was discovered on the day of the super moon, the fullest moon of the century so far. Interestingly, it happened to be the same day as Cinco de Mayo. Steve Graham and I share credit for the naming it Ciudad Luna. Good name, but no idea if it will stick.

This project has had layers of inexplicable "coincidences" for decades. Captain Steve Morgan, as well as many indigenous people, have for years attributed the flow of events related to Ciudad Blanca to the power of the monkey gods. Hurricanes, the sudden deaths of explorers and archaeologists, the paralyzing fears of the locals and now this project are all a part of the legend. With this venture, the mystical beliefs of Mabel, Bruce, Lobo, and Africo play a role in how we wound up being able to pull it off. The universe works in strange and wondrous ways.

•

Late in the afternoon, **Africo Madrid** arrived from **Tegucigalpa** and greeted the military minions who had been stationed at the airport. He will stay with us at Parrot Tree and join us

for a dinner party on the beach.

Tomorrow, Africo looks at the computer and gets a sampling of the LiDAR findings in several different spots which have similar appearance and structural components. He is 100% primed to believe in the accuracy and it seems pretty certain to me that he will become even more enthusiastic after the demo in Michael's room

followed by questions and answers with Steve, Bill, me and whoever else is around.

Not to de-emphasize why we're here, tomorrow will also most likely be the last day of flying. Chuck and Juan will concentrate on the area between the targets, the hills and valleys they are interested in between **T1** and **T3**.

Tomorrow night, a party is being hosted by

Africo and the President—though he probably won't be here—for our whole party plus the governor of Roatan and who knows who else.

We all have reservations to fly to Houston—on the same plane, I think—at 1 PM on Saturday. Then we'll split up. The Houston guys will stay. Garry and Bill and the documentary crew will go to LAX. I'll go to Chicago and Doug will go to Santa Fe. Brad will go back to Washington D.C.

It seems that Steve, Mabel and Bruce will stick around Tegucigalpa for the official announcement by the President and/or Virgilio on Monday or Tuesday. We will make our announcement—with the same story—at the same time. After that, hold on to your hats—the winds of change will be blowing hard.

#16 Africo Likes It!
Friday 12, 2012
Last update in Roatan, Bay Islands, Honduras

At 9:30 AM, behind the curtain in Michael Sartori's room, the first non-crew unveiling of what we've been doing on this project.

The primary audience, **Carlos Africo Madrid Hart**, his mother Carole Hart and Virgilio Paredes was transfixed for nearly an hour. All of it was recorded in real time as Commander Elkins, our CEO Bill Benenson and Doug Preston, the most able articulator of archaeological context in our group, looked at Michael's laptop as he demonstrated what LiDAR hath wrought.

Michael made it happen on the box. Steve also did much of the explaining. The Honduran honcho listened and stared intently. Africo asked a bunch of questions. Some answers, whether from Steve, Bill, or Doug were interpreted by his mother.

In particular the session was built around our findings, starting with a shot of the canopy, then a screen showing the dot clouds underneath, and then focusing on various images that demonstrate what's actually on the ground.

Michael was able to show evidence of what we all believe to be clusters of very old city or village life – seen on-screen as squares that are probably the tops of pyramids or other large buried, step-like features, pathways and other indications of the relationship between the features and the topography – down to a few centimeters which transmogrify the perspective of the images to see it from a ground's-eye or other points-of-view that make the features clearer.

It was a remarkable session. And the video we shot captures the first semi-formal articulation of our high-stakes 21st-century exploration successes.

Of course, Africo and Virgilio say they understand that this is only the beginning of a long process of discovery but they again made it absolutely clear that they want to get in there ASAP. After the session over a glass of white wine at the Palapa, Africo said he would like to get into the place he saw at **T1** in a helicopter, perhaps immediately after the press conference early next week.

"It's a free country," as we used to say as kids—though in this case it might be more apt to say, "It's his and President "Pepe" Lobo's country." They can do what they want.

It doesn't seem like we'll be here if they go next week. While it's definitely a long shot that they will be able to land, or even get close enough to actually see any ground-truth in the next week or two, whatever happens in "our" areas are and will continue to be "our" story. We must be present at the traditional moment of discovery to document it. And, we will be there. But tomorrow, none of us will be here.

It was a true celebration at the bash Africo threw at Gio's for us, the mayor, the Roatan governor (who owns the Ace Hardware store —the biggest in Bay Islands), and a few other local muckety-mucks.

The dinner with Africo's mother Carole, Bill, Bruce, Mabel, Doug, and Steve all seated at the round table was a huge success. Africo has the presence and grace of a charismatic leader. He's also really smart. He speaks and understands most of just about everything that's being said to him in English. When he didn't, he looked across the table to "Mama," and she was always ready to explain the nuances. She has been a translator for many years in Florida. He knew when it was important enough to have a full understanding of what Bill or Steve or Doug was saying. Impressive guy who absolutely welcomed our group of more than a dozen to his country and expressed clearly

how significant our contribution and work was to him and to Honduras. Virgilio and Garry sat together and reached consensus on the way to write and present the press release and public posturing. Of course the final judgments and decision-making rests with Africo and the President, but the table is set to do a joint release and literally be on the same page.

The evening concluded with Africo saying "We welcome you to our country. We are grateful to you. We know this is the first step of wonderful things to come."

He is pumped about the good-news historical happening on his watch—almost all of which he frequently attributes to the wondrous work of God.

Who are we to argue?

After the party we went back for our last night at Parrot Tree, had a nightcap and prepared for our trip back to the USA.

#17 Back to "Civilization"
Saturday February 13, 2012

By 8 AM we had packed our bags, put them on the bus and had our last breakfast at Parrot Tree. I'd recommend it to any tourist. We were a jolly group. It kind of reminded me of the ride after winning a basketball game at a rival school. The experience is a whole lot better than when you lose. None of us had lost. We had definitely succeeded and we were on our way back to our families and lives.

We had eaten well, been outdoors by the sea. We all were healthy and had made a bunch of new, talented and interesting friends.

As we headed to the airport in Roatan (again) I surprised the group by handing out T-shirts I had made in Chicago. Little things mean a lot —everyone was happy to have this one-of-a-kind shirt as a badge of their accomplishments.

PART THREE: BACK IN THE USA

En route Chicago
Saturday, May 10, 2012

We were finished in **Roatan**. The work on the LiDAR imaging will continue for a long time, but we're on our way back home. United to Houston at 1:05 is loaded with UTL'ers—maybe a baker's dozen. **Chuck Gross** is flying the Cessna back to Houston, after a stop to pick up the GPS units and, I think, to drop **Juan Carlos** in Tegucigalpa to catch up with family.

Mabel & Bruce Heinicke and **Steve Elkins** will have a Mother's Day dinner tomorrow in Tegoose and then a 4 PM Monday meeting at **IHAH** to prepare for the Presidential press conference on Tuesday, including creating a PowerPoint. At the Presidential Palace, our group and the Honduran dignitaries will make the official announcement of the small step we have taken for mankind.

Juan Carlos will likely be there also, though he apparently has ambivalent feelings about becoming too high profile in his country. Since he knows the precise locations of everything, he has some fear that in this Wild West country he might be subject to attention and perhaps even threats that he doesn't need to subject himself to. Fascinating irony for a guy Doug Preston has characterized as a probable national hero—the discoverer of a lost city in the **Mosquitia**, if not the legendary **Lost City of Ciudad Blanca**. It will be interesting to see how Juan's situation plays out—and of course, what happens with the Commander, the Prez, the US Ambassador and most especially the media reactions at and after Wednesday's event.

At the same hour on Wednesday, in Southern California, **UTL/Benenson Productions**, through its publicist, will issue a press release, unleashing global media attention, the first stage of what Bill has called "the explosion." It will be fascinating to see how that plays out in the next week or so also.

Are we too close to it? Is what we have sweet enough to attract swarms of media bees? How long will it take? What will happen before **Doug Preston's** proposal to *The New Yorker* is accepted and published? What kind of media buzz will his article create? And will anyone much care about the miracle of LiDAR discovery in an obscure jungle in Honduras, or will the real explosion not happen until we have incontrovertible physical proof of discovery?

Just like this whole passionate adventure, for almost 20 years now, nobody knows all the answers.

My Story And I'm Sticking To It
Wednesday, May 16, 2012
Chicago, Illinois

I'm finally back in Chicago after a month in the Caribbean—ten days in Corn Island off Nicaragua and then almost three weeks at a Roatan resort, headquarters for our crew. We became the first people to track a lost city beneath the Mosquitia jungle canopy—or any other—with airborne laser imaging systems (LiDAR).

Living with them we were in nearly an ego-free zone. Everyone had his strengths and didn't want to tread on anyone else. Plus, we had absolutely comfortable single suites to go to whenever we needed.

We had three LiDAR technicians from Houston. **Juan Carlos Fernandez Diaz**, a rock-steady engineer/pilot with a cute sense of humor and refreshing thirst for knowledge. He flew in the cramped Cessna on every mission. **Michael Sartori** was more gruff on the outside, but experienced and blessed with intelligence and a taste for irony. **Abhinav Singhania**, a younger tech expert, is skilled at patiently manipulating the imagery to make the abstract more concrete.

On the image-making side, we had three video/still production guys from LA who documented the entire process: **Steve Graham**, a good-guy dedicated cameraman whose skill at capturing process developed over the time we were there; **Mark Adams**, the most outgoing and considerate of all our crew, a skilled field audio man and helpful production contributor every day; and **Roberto Ysias**, who never tired of seeing people, objects and places through his still camera lens and told fascinating stories of his shoots all over the world.

Perhaps the best and brightest was **Douglas Preston**, a best-selling novelist, journalist and nonfiction writer who has written at least 25 books and will be writing our story, first for *The New Yorker* and then likely as a nonfiction book.

The two most unique characters were probably **Bruce** and **Mabel Heinicke** who functioned as the Honduran logistics and connections coordinators. They had stories and lives that were absolutely fascinating. **Mango Hernandez** is Mabel's brother, a Honduran football hero and a reliable guy who did what was asked of him.

Then there was our pilot, **Charles Gross III**

from Florida, a genuine character who served four years in Iraq, using this same sophisticated LiDAR technology to identify military targets, not archaeology sites.

We already know lots about our leader and my long-time partner in seeking this lost city, **Steve Elkins**. He saw everything that was going on and had the rare ability to anticipate what was about to happen, whether with the crew, the science, or the video production. After a while, we were joined by the executive producer and director of the documentary, **Bill Benenson**, who put up (or got) the cash to make it all possible—he had it but didn't flaunt it. Bill's LA pal, **Garry Spire** did all he could to help move it all in a sensible direction—incongruous for a project that frequently made no logical sense.

And then there was me—a generally affable observer, chronicler and quiet influencer of people and production.

For much of the time, **Virgilio Paredes** was with us. As the head of the Honduran Institute of Anthropology and History he was our connection to authority, though he seldom forced an issue other than lunch.

Last weekend, the Secretary of Interior, the guy who seems to be the #2 official in the Honduran government, **Carlos Africo Madrid Hart**, joined us and was thrilled with the results of our research and on our last night, hosted a Honduran-style banquet.

Quite a group. All good diligent guys who were good at what they did. But, all guys who worked hard to make the project a success. It didn't hurt that we were staying on a beautiful

Caribbean bay in a really nice first-class resort, **Parrot Tree Beach Resort**.

We were from everywhere, but lived in peace in our little global village.

I was busy some 16 hours a day—helping to coordinate the production and logistics, directing and being part of lots of video shooting and interviewing—mostly of our group as the process of searching unfolded—and writing a private journal/blog/history for Steve, Bill, and Doug plus NCALM, my family, and other interested parties to consume every day and for archival uses in the future. I scribbled notes nearly all day, every day, and usually constructed the chronicles on my laptop late at night—10 PM to 2 AM—my usual writing hours at home.

I also made time to jump in the sea nearly every day—usually an early AM swim, sometimes a sunset dip, plus an occasional snorkel.

All in all, a terrific experience, mostly because we were able to accomplish the dream that Steve and I have been pursuing since the mid-90s. We DID make history by applying this laser-mapping technology to uncover and discover evidence of human ruins in places that no 20th-century people have ever been (as far as we know).

You just can't get there on land, through the incredibly thick, formidable, and dangerous jungle. When we go, it will have to be by helicopter.

•

The Presidential Palace, Tegucigalpa – May 12, 2012

I have to believe that if today's announcement by Honduran President **Profirio Lobo Sosa** and officials in Tegucigalpa, speaking alongside my long-time pal and partner, Steve Elkins—identified on national TV and print as "Dr. Helkins Steve"—is a good indicator, this story will continue to have lots of ramifications. It's like a peeling onion with a life of its own and we figure to be heavily involved as it keeps going.

The company that Bill Benenson controls, UTL (for Under The LiDAR) has a contract with the government for all rights in all media for this project of exploration. The people/government of Honduras, of course, retain all rights to everything that's there and will ever be discovered. So far, so good.

Actually quite remarkable—a script we couldn't have written and a future we can't predict.

Where From Here?
Thursday May 18, 2012
Chicago, Illinois

Our scientist-cohorts at the **National Center for Airborne Laser Mapping** (NCALM) at the University of Houston and Berkeley will continue to manipulate the data and come up with more detailed information on what's there - including likely sites that we/they haven't found yet among the renderings.

They will also determine logical locations —breaks in the canopy—where a helicopter could land or hover to drop our military guys in to clear a landing place. Then, whenever that is—days, weeks, months—our Honduran government partners and we will go there to check out the **"ground-truth"** in the locations we have identified with LiDAR as most likely to contain ruins such as pyramids, temples, ball courts, and other related ancient city-like features.

Of course, all of that process will be documented on video and become chapters of our documentary.

There are a million complications that I won't begin to go into here. But, suffice to say, Honduras is like a combination of Dodge City and Al Capone's Chicago with the highest per capita murder rate of any country in the world. The drug cartels with their money and influence dominate much of "civic" life.

The government and military are inextricably intertwined with US military forces and the DEA which now says a vast amount of the drug trafficking that used to go through Mexican narcos is now centered in Honduras and in the Mosquitia in particular. In general, Honduras has the poorest population anywhere in the Americas, after Haiti.

I must say that I experienced the people as genuine, accepting and generous. I felt the same way twice in the last ten years visiting Cuba where people didn't have anything, but were unquestionably open, unresentful and happy to make direct personal connections. And music everywhere.

So our (possible) discovery of **Ciudad Blanca**, the legendary **Lost City** that disappeared in the jungle, is seen as a potential boost for Honduras – a hopeful sign in a place where good news reports are few and far between.

We have no proof that what we have uncovered is, in fact, a remnant of an ancient civilization. But, we do know that some artifacts and remains in areas close-by have been carbon-dated as far back as 3000 B.C.—way before the flowering of the Mayans or Aztecs.

Who they were and how they disappeared before the evidence was swallowed up by the jungle remains a mystery.

Historically, the indigenous people who live in the Mosquitia villages have been scared to death of "what's up there" in the currently uninhabited jungle. It has been speculated by various archaeologists and anthropologists that the people who were there built one large capital, a trading city, with smaller satellite cities nearby. The legend has persisted for centuries that they worshipped "monkey gods," similar to **Hanuman**, the Hindu monkey god. Many still believe valuable treasures are there. At this point, it's 100% speculation. No evidence has surfaced for centuries.

We do know that we have been able to begin a new era, a revolution, in archaeological research methodology. It doesn't require shlepping through god-awful, virtually impossible terrain for weeks or months at a time, places loaded with deadly poisonous snakes and spiders, insects, bats, jaguars and other creatures—and who knows what?

We also know that many people over the years have tried to get there and didn't return. Some who perished were academics— allegedly including a group of archaeologists from University of Pennsylvania in the 1950's. Some were treasure seekers who believed the tales and legends about mountains of gold and jewels up there.

Whatever happens, the next era of discovery is likely to take decades. The first task is to try to unravel the mysteries of these places that nobody knew or had located until last week.

The one thing we have done is to find sites without damaging them as we "discovered" them—archaeology by the numbers, if you will.

We have been sitting in resort rooms, ruminating over data and renderings, rather than doing reconnaissance by machete, dependent on fires and dodging mosquitoes.

Our survival involved fresh lobsters and steamed kingfishers, not hunting and gathering to kill snakes and vermin to eat. I prefer it our way!

Anyway, that's a small glimpse at what's been happening these past few weeks.

Now That I'm Home And Get Asked About The Trip...
Monday, May 22, 2012
Chicago, Illinois

Here's how I describe it to regular people: "This fukkin' LiDAR is amazing!"

We were able to penetrate the jungle canopy—50 meters deep in many places—and "see" evidence of human settlement in locations that Steve and our team have been thinking likely for 17 years. In fact, it's in the very valley I checked out in a military helicopter back in 1998.

We have only raw data, renderings, and indications at the moment. We'll need lots more processing. No way to tell how old, or anything else definitive about the physical evidence, or even that it is THE Lost City of legend. Probably, there is no singular "**Lost City of Ciudad Blanca**," but a bunch of places—none of which any modern people have seen—yet.

The Rest Of 2012

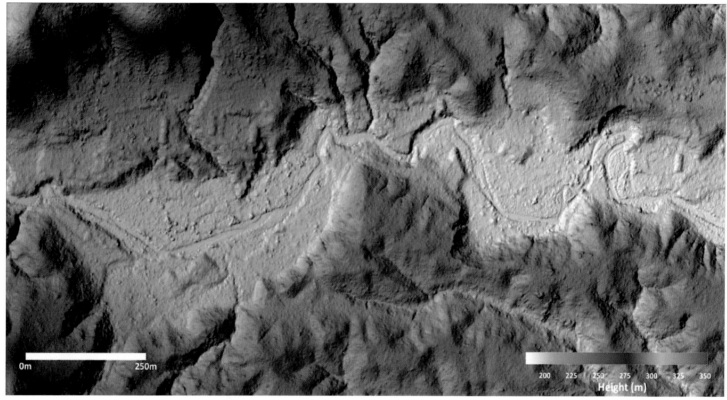

0m   250m

200   225   250   275   300   325   350
Height (m)

We wound up spending the next two and a half years preparing for the expedition to go into the jungle for the ground-truthing of what we had documented on LiDAR.

For months, the **NCALM** guys in Houston, especially **Juan Carlos**, **Bill Carter** and the director **Ramesh Shrestha**, constantly massaged the LiDAR data to further define what's there, with emphasis on **T1** and **T3**, the most promising locations for relics and structures.

Everyone who was or might be part of the jungle expedition stayed in constant touch with Steve Elkins. He was full-time taking care of business arrangements, logistics, and technical details, constantly dealing with Bill Benenson and his Chief Operating Officer, **Wendi Weger** in Santa Monica.

Later in 2012, **Chris Fisher** came aboard. A professor at Colorado State University, he was a rare combination of Meso-American archae-ologist/anthropologist and an experienced in-terpreter of LiDAR data. He had been working on a project using ground LiDAR at a relatively unknown ruin in **Michoacan, Mexico.** Our proj-ect was a logical extension of his work. He embraced it and got into it with both feet. I doubt there's anyone in the world with his experience, drive and knowledge. He really knows his stuff. I'm a believer. Plus, he's an affable fun guy, as long as you stay on the right side of him, professionally and personally.

•

There were so many parts of the puzzle to solve and prepare. Steve and Bill concluded that it made sense to get everyone in the same room to share our individual knowledge and to communicate the planning we had done for the next phases. We wound up having a meeting in a San Francisco hotel conference room on December 7, 2012, bringing together 18 people for eight hours.

It included ten PhDs—experts in archaeology, LiDAR, satellite mapping, anthropology, and earth sciences, among others. Author **Doug Preston**, conferenced in via Skype from his home in Santa Fe for most of the day. As with almost every step of our process, we documented it on video for eventual use in our documentary, for archival record and to show to team members who would join later. For many months, we were trying to learn as much as we could in order to develop the strategy and techniques that would give us the best chance for success once we were at the site in the jungle.

Four "outsiders" joined us in the hotel conference room: **Ben Kacyra**, founder of CyArk, a non-profit dedicated to the protection of culture and history across the globe using ground LiDAR; **Liz Lee**, CyArk chief of operations; **Dan Thompson**, satellite mapping expert from Stanford and Global Heritage Network; and **George Rossman**, distinguished earth sciences expert from Cal Tech and Steve's neighbor in Pasadena.

By the end of the day, it was clear that we were on our way to evolving a viable ongoing operating plan to go to the jungle in the months ahead. We became more real. Nearly everyone signed nondisclosure agreements. **Garry Spire** was Bill's representative. Shortly after that, Bill reaffirmed his commitment to take financial responsibility for the ground-truthing project and the documentary to be made about it.

San Francisco, December 7, 2012. L to R: Archaeologist **Dan Thompson**; Professor **George Rossman** of Caltech; **Bill Carter** of NCALM; NCALM Director **Ramesh Shrestha**; **Juan Carlos Fernandez Diaz** of NCALM; author **Doug Preston** (on monitor); archaeologist **Chris Fisher** and his research partner, geographer **Steve Leisz**; **Steve Elkins**; anthropologist **Alicia Gonzalez**; producer **Garry Spire** representing Bill and UTL.

THE EL DORADO MACHINE

A new scanner's rain-forest discoveries.

By Douglas Preston

The rain forests of Mosquitia, which span more than thirty-two thousand square miles of Honduras and Nicaragua, are among the densest and most inhospitable in the world. "It's mountainous," Chris Begley, an archeologist and expert on Honduras, told me recently. "There's white water. There are jumping vipers, coral snakes, fer-de-lance, stinging plants, and biting insects. And then there are the illnesses—malaria, dengue fever, leishmaniasis, Chagas'." Nevertheless, for nearly a century, archeologists and adventurers have plunged into the region, in search of the ruins of an ancient city, built of white stone, called la Ciudad Blanca, the White City.

Pre-Columbian jungles were far more densely populated than once thought.

Illustration by Ron Kurniawan

Rumors of the site's existence date back at least to 1526, when, in a letter to the Spanish emperor Charles V, the conquistador Hernán Cortés reported hearing "reliable" information about a province in the interior of Honduras that "will exceed Mexico in riches, and equal it in the largeness of its towns and villages." The claim was not an impossible one; the New World encountered by Europeans had wealthy cities and evidence of former splendor. In 1839, John Lloyd Stephens, an American diplomat and amateur archeologist, went in search of a group of ruins in the jungles of western Honduras—and found the stupendous remains of the Maya city of Copán, which he bought from a local landowner for fifty dollars. Stephens explored scores of other iconic ruins in Central America, which he described in a lavishly illustrated, best-selling book; serious archeology soon followed. Researchers have since determined that, beginning around 250 B.C., much of Mesoamerica south of Mexico had been dominated by the Maya civilization, which held sway until its mysterious collapse, in the tenth century.

Into 2013

The early months of 2013 were spent scurrying around team-building and finding the best ways to efficiently put the details of archaeology, video, and jungle logistics together. It moved to a new plateau in May. In its May 6, 2013 issue, *The New Yorker* published **Doug Preston**'s long and impressive article that spurred enormous global media and scientific interest in our project. The story covered the legend, the historical and cultural context in Honduras, the scientific implications of LiDAR in archaeology, our team and unique experience. Preston was the only non-aviator who squeezed into the Cessna with Chuck Gross, the pilot, Juan Carlos and the millions of dollars in LiDAR equipment.

The article was headlined **"The El Dorado Machine."** The story and the credibility of *The New Yorker* fueled huge interest about us and the project. Within days, headlines all over the world speculated about the implications of our LiDAR expedition. This continued for years.

89

The internet stories got out of control quickly. That's the first time I understood first-hand the power of internet information and social media and how it can absolutely distort.

We had correspondence from every continent after Doug's article. Steve, Chris Fisher and I—on a local basis—were approached to do radio, TV and print appearances.

In early 2013, the Honduran officials needed to have a proper and public acknowledgment of the expedition we were going to do together. Steve and anthropologist **Alicia Gonzalez** made a trip to Tegucigalpa to meet with Cabinet Minister **Africo Madrid Hart** and **Virgilio Paredes**, head of the Honduran Institute for History and Anthropology (IHAH), to sign papers with the Institute for our expedition.

Steve and Alicia spent some research time in its museum and after going through all the files about missions into the Mosquitia, they were satisfied that nobody had ever taken out a permit or done any scientific reporting on the exact area we had isolated on the LiDAR.

They did learn a bunch about prior expeditions that they/we didn't know about before, many to locations near our valley, but nothing in the exact spot in the dense jungle.

On October 18, I got this **email** from Steve:

Bill and I each got this today. Preston is writing a 700-word article for them about the project. Who would have thought I would become a "Global Thinker".

- Steve

Begin forwarded message:
From: Global Thinkers <Globalthinkers@ foreignpolicy.com>
Subject: Foreign Policy magazine's Leading Global Thinkers
Date: October 18, 2013 2:23:15 PM PDT
Dear Mr. Steve Elkins,

*It is my pleasure to congratulate you on your selection as one of **Foreign Policy's Leading Global Thinkers of 2013**. The editors of Foreign Policy chose you based on your standout contributions over the last year—your ability to translate important ideas into action.*

We will be highlighting you and your work in our next issue, to be published in December, and on our website, foreignpolicy.com. In addition to a short biography of you and each of the other Leading Global Thinkers.

... To celebrate our Global Thinkers and all they have accomplished, we are pleased to invite you to join us in Washington on December 11. A detailed formal invitation for a full day of events involving our Global Thinkers and a large, influential audience from Washington and around the world will follow. During the day, we will be presenting a program looking at global developments and the year ahead which will feature keynote remarks by U.S. Secretary of State John Kerry, as well as other senior American officials, diplomats, and business leaders.

There will also be a major evening reception honoring you and your fellow thinkers which has become one of the most prominent such events to take place in Washington each winter. Last year, more than half of our thinkers joined us from around the world, and we hope you will be among them for this year's ceremonies. A member of our staff will be following up with you shortly to see how we can help with arrangements.

Again, congratulations on your selection. We hope to hear from you at your earliest convenience, and we look forward to seeing you in December.
Sincerely,
J. Peter Scoblic
Executive Editor, Analysis and Commentary

•

The event in December 2013, in Washington and the momentum from being named Leading Global Thinkers was good karma and helped propel the project toward the next steps.

Our finances for the expedition and production were undetermined before that, but, as a Global Thinker, Bill committed to take full responsibility for the money needed for exploration and documentation.

It was then definite—we would find a way to go into the Mosquitia by 2015!

Steve and I were convinced we would see for ourselves what was there and produce a documentary about it. What we found changed world history just a bit.

The preparation process was fraught with details, logistics and a few seeming dead ends. Lots of phone calls and emails, long discussions and negotiations with scientists, suppliers, helicopter charters, Latin American fixers, security people and video dealers followed

Plenty of stops and starts—frustrations and exhilarations. Steve was always in the middle of it. We spoke about it and emailed every day.

In Houston, the **NCALM** group along with Chris Fisher in Colorado and Steve continued to manipulate the data, preparing for the ground-truthing expedition into the jungle to determine if what we had discovered with the LiDAR could actually be found and the best way to do it.

They were particularly interested in target **T3**. The more the scientists studied the data and maps, the more it looked like a full-blown ancient city that appeared to include roads, a ball court, 100-foot mounds that might well have been covering earthen pyramids and land that had been manipulated for agriculture.

Like **T1**, **T3** was undisturbed, un-deforested and unlooted. It was significantly larger than **T1**. Chris Fisher called **T3** a significant ancient city that covered more area than **Copán**, the largest and most famous reconstructed Mayan ruin in Honduras. He wanted to go there first. But for years, Elkins and I had assumed that the first location to check out would be **T1**, the site we had been tracking since 1995.

NCALM, Houston - **Steve Elkins** (right) with Professor **George Rossman** of Caltech and **Michael Sartori**

A simian sculpture on Temple 11 in **Copán** possibly representing howler monkey gods

•

Planning The Expedition

UTL Production Office, Santa Monica, CA. L to R: **Sparky Greene**, coordinating producer; **Wendi Wegner,** COO Benenson Productions; **Steve Elkins; Julie Trompush** (obscured), Benenson Productions Coordinator; **Bill Benenson**

By November 2014, with our logistics getting worked out in some detail and a go-date planned for February 14, 2015, I started to realize that the part I knew the most about —producing documentary TV—seemed to be getting lost in the shuffle.

Steve had lined up an experienced video camera guy with great support from **Mark Adams**, a wonderful all-purpose audio guy who was with us in Roatan and had Bill's and Steve's 100% trust for years. They were topflight mainstream documentary film/video

makers. But the documentary I envisioned went beyond the mainstream, reflecting my own unique experience and point of view.

I have lived with the historical value of nonfiction video as perhaps no other producer, creating and maintaining the **Media Burn**

Independent Video Archive (*mediaburn.org*), that has been seen by 16 million online visitors in the last ten years. So, I was keenly aware of the significance of the whole body of documentary material that's produced for an unprecedented project like this—even though most of the footage is never seen publicly in a film or TV show.

I wanted this jungle adventure and production process to incorporate "my kind of TV." I knew it would take some convincing—and negotiating—to get it to happen.

Bill had financial control of the entire project. He had produced Hollywood features and some truly well-done documentaries. Understandably, he had tremendous anxiety about the responsibilities and safety requirements for involving some 20 people in an unknown jungle environment in a politically dangerous and unpredictable country.

I knew what I wanted to do. I needed to articulate it. I pitched a documentary called *"Our Gang"* to be incorporated as part of the documentary Benenson Productions was planning to produce. I wrote a plan for doing the doc-within-a-doc and presented it to Bill and Steve. (See **Notes**.)

Steve understood it and endorsed it almost immediately. Even after Bill and I sat for an hour in his office, he wouldn't take that leap of faith.

"Our Gang" never happened. It would have required sending another videographer to shoot with me. Bill saw that as more of a burden than a benefit. I was disappointed, not just for me but for the strength of the collaborative film we could make.

The path to the discoveries has never been straight. The external realities, politics, and logistics seemed unending. Internally, we had our detours as well. Putting together the best possible production team took some finagling, mostly because of settling on dates and having people commit. Nothing is real until it is—in this case, until we had everyone on the plane to Tegucigalpa. That's a lesson I've learned from 40 or so years of producing and having the "firm plans" melt into Jell-O. Actually, it's a near-miracle we did wind up in the jungle in February 2015.

Even Bill had major stops and starts—three or four that I can remember in the five months of "final" lead-up. Understandably, Bill—along with his wife, **Laurie**—went back and forth, thinking it would all be too much and deciding to abort the whole mission, only to decide days, or sometimes only hours later that we HAD to go.

We set a target date for the entire group to meet in Houston on Valentine's Day, 2015. Everyone—all 20 of us—cleared our schedules, made our deals with Steve and peace with our families. The equipment, supplies, insurance, plane tickets, hotels—in Houston, **Tegucigalpa** and **Catacamas**, transportation in Honduras,

The Lost City Gang comes together, Houston, October 2014

L to R: **Dr. Juan Carlos Fernandez Diaz**, NCALM; the author; Archaeologist **Dr. Chris Fisher**, Colorado State University; **Wendi Weger**, COO Benenson Productions; Honduran Secretary of the Interior **Africo Madrid Hart**; **Steve Elkins**, our jefé; Anthropologist and Latin American expert **Dr. Alicia M. Gonzales**; and security and logistics professional **Al Edgington.**

95

political and military arrangements, and hundreds of other pieces were all put in place.

And best we could, we made our individual peace with the monkey gods we barely knew. That legend persisted, frequently as a joke, but it was never far from our consciousness. One of the scientists confided that every time he got on a plane or helicopter, he made a small offering for good luck to the monkey gods. Like the rest of us, he felt there was no downside to acknowledging them—just in case!

•

Bill Benenson is cautious by nature—an anomaly for a guy who takes enormous risks, like making a movie in the most fearsome jungle in the continent. My guess is that this venture was probably more of a leap into the unknown than any of his other film or business deals. He had one last "I-just-can't-do it" moment 13 days before we were all scheduled to fly to Honduras. Too much seemed unresolved on designated departure minus 13 days. He had to work it out.

Sparky Greene, Malibu business maven, author and entrepreneur, served as Bill's consigliere during the final weeks before we left and in the two weeks in 2015 in Honduras. Sparky, Bill and I spent five hours on the beautiful Benenson patio in Santa Monica just two weeks before the whole group was scheduled to leave for Honduras and the jungle. Bill almost called it all off. There was too much uncertainty.

Sparky and I understood why Bill had doubts. The helicopter situation was edgy and without fail-safe backup. The original schedule had been moved forward several weeks in order to accommodate the availability of the British ex-Special Air Services officers. But they hadn't been reached directly and were spread around the globe on three different jungle assignments.

Finally, after the long discussion with us and spending time with Laurie, Bill was convinced there was little choice but to proceed as planned. After a phone conversation with Steve, who told him in no uncertain terms that he would have to call the whole thing off forever if Bill tried to postpone it, the deal was sealed.

We would leave in two weeks for two weeks in Honduras. It was inviolate. Let the chips fall where they may. We'd all make it work somehow or other.

And we were off to the races.

The Final Plan—Best I Can Predict Today

Santa Monica, CA
February 2, 2015

• Feb 14—Group gathers in Houston.

• Feb 15—Flight from Houston to **Tegucigalpa**.

• Feb 16—Nice coach to **Catacamas**. 3-4 hrs. with about 18 of us. We take over Hotel Papabeto in Catacamas for the duration.

• Feb 17—Helicopter takes off for first trip to the jungle site. Find landing place—or build it—in what Africo Madrid, our Honduran connection wants to call "**The Valley of the Jaguar.**" Set up camp.

• Shuttle people back & forth to the site via helicopter—30-40 mins per trip.

• We'll have at least 16 people working at the camp site for about 10-12 days: the video crew; *National Geographic* photographer and writer; two US archaeologists; one Honduran archaeologist; a cultural anthropologist, ground LiDAR survey engineer; three British Special Forces guys who take care of camp, logistics, security, medical, communications; and three producer-director types, including me.

• And we'll have Honduran military guys with big guns both at the site in jungle and at Catacamas.

Pretty crazy, huh?

We will likely go to at least a second known jungle site about 25 miles away and perhaps a third if we can.

On or about March 2, we'll go back to Tegucigalpa and hold a press conference—probably on March 3 or 4—hosted by the President of Honduras.

I hope to be home and safe and healthy by Thursday or Friday, March 5 or 6.

Hard to believe. Food will be MRE military-type stuff in the jungle. I expect I'll be able to get to Catacamas at least once, maybe twice for a shower, a meal, a beer or Coke, and a real bed – but not sure.

That's it. Simple.

PART FOUR: CHRONICLES 2015—OUR JUNGLE ADVENTURE

#1 Tegucigalpa, Here We Come!
February 14, 2015
Tegucigalpa, Honduras

Today was about more than anticipation—it was the beginning of a buzz, both for what we're here to do and for who we are.

6:00 AM call at the hotel, and the flight, **Houston-Tegucigalpa**, went without a hitch.

United Air Lines took good care of us, marking, and checking 40-something pieces of luggage and gear for ten of us. All of us and our stuff made it to the capital of Honduras a bit after noon.

Virgilio Paredes Trapero of the Honduran Institute of Anthropology and History (IHAH) and Colonel Willy Joe Oseguera of the Honduran military set up a private immigration procedure in the airport's VIP lounge.

We were in that lounge for close to an hour. It was air-conditioned and way more comfortable than any place in the airport. We had time for our gang to get acquainted.

It was an unusually experienced, competent and interesting group of characters.

Some 100 finger prints, 40 thumbprints, and 20 digital photos later, our passports were stamped. We were all legal in Honduras.

Five of us had been on the Roatan LiDAR adventure in 2012:

Commander **Steve Elkins**,

Soundman **Mark Adams**,

author **Doug Preston**,

Juan Carlos Fernandez Diaz of NCALM,

and yours truly, the official Chronicler.

Iain "Spud" Mathesen,

We were joined in Tegucigalpa by the rest of our team of specialists:

Andrew "Woody" Wood,

and **Stevie "Sully" Sullivan,** all former British Special Air Service members in charge of our security and logistics.

Our archaeological team:

Chris Fisher, Lead Archaeologist,

Anna Cohen, Field Archaeologist,

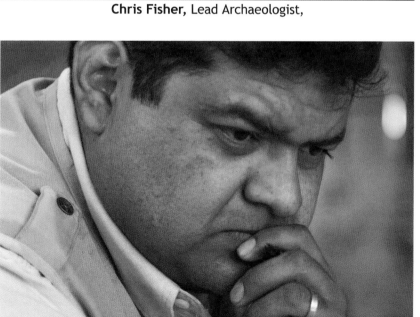

Oscar Neil Cruz, IHAH Archaeologist,

and **Alicia Gonzalez**, Anthropologist and Latin American specialist.

The rest of our group included:

Lucian Read, Director of Photography,

Myles Elsing, our helicopter pilot,

Josh Feezer, camera assistant and media wrangler,

Jeff Adams, helicopter mechanic,

Dave Yoder, photographer on assignment from *National Geographic*,

Maritza Carbajal, our translator and fixer extraordinaire,

Julie Trompush, Benenson Productions Coordinator,

and **Sparky Greene**, Coordinating Producer.

While we were in Immigration, the *National Geographic* team of writer **Doug Preston** and photographer **Dave Yoder** met for first time. Dave showed us the Pope Francis photo he took on Christmas Day, 2014. In full regalia and ultra-powerful, looking forward, the solo image in the Vatican is set to be on the cover of NatGeo. It's a classic and I'd bet, soon-to-be-prize-winning photo.

Lucian recorded the whole day's process on video, from Houston to the VIP room where we

had an initial and thorough security briefing by **Iain "Spud" Mathesen**, one of three **TAFF**s (Television & Film Facilitation Services), who will be with us the entire time.

Andrew "Woody" Wood is the ranking officer and **Stevie "Sully" Sullivan** is the third Brit. It feels as if we're in good hands. They're calm, firm, communicate clearly in the Queen's English and seem comfortable taking

full responsibility for our safety.

Steve Elkins—aka "Dr. Helkins"—did a five-minute backgrounder on the 20+ years of our fascination with the Lost City chase and how it evolved with **Bill Benenson**'s financial commitment.

Steve's talk was first directed at the helicopter pilot **Myles Elsing**, and mechanic **Jeff Adams**, who had just arrived. Myles could not be mistaken for anything other than an aviation veteran—by looks, manner and fresh petrol smell. They had just arrived from their three-day trip from New Mexico. The only minor hang-up was a little heat by officials in Tampico, Mexico for one bureaucratic reason or another. Myles has a face-wide white mustache and has been around—and around again for 1000's of helicopter and fixed-wing flying missions. He'll be piloting dozens of **Catacamas**—jungle round-trips in the next two weeks. Jeff will likely spend those days in the well-protected "home" of the heli, making sure it stays 100%.

The Honduran military chopper is a key factor in the project for moving their people and our stuff around and for the initial landing and set-up of the base camp. Using it will also permit us to document our process from the air. Sparky assured them that we are there not just to cooperate as "guests" but to help the interests of the people and ecology of the country.

After 45 minutes or so, several people were dismissed and the Honduran colonel, plus his pilot and four younger military personnel stayed in the conference room with us. A detailed discussion ensued with large maps of the site laid out on table and the interchange between the Honduran helicopter crew and security people and our group. Steve, Chris Fisher and Juan Carlos showed the possible landing sites which they have spent dozens of

hours determining with the LiDAR data. They discussed and demonstrated the possibilities and logistics as we've come to know them.

The military helicopter requires a larger landing spot, so where to go and the required time and distance to get to our area of interest is intertwined with where we land and set up base camp. It will likely be resolved within the next 48 hours.

We'll all bus cross-country on Sunday morning to Catacamas—about four hours—with a full complement of military personnel. Monday will be test-rappelling in Catacamas for the special forces guys to do, assuming the heli and fuel allow. Then, doing the initial reconnaissance fly-over the **T1** site—still otherwise unbranded at this point.

Our goal is to get down on the ground and set up our base camp as soon as practicable—Tuesday, Wednesday? It obviously depends on the nature of the landing site, how far away it is, safety considerations, etc.

The evening brought a reception at the U.S. **Ambassador James Nealon**'s house, a 10,000 square foot hilltop mansion behind triple thick glass with major military protection. I wasn't part of the delegation, but by all reports, it was cordial, and encouraging. The ambassador, who had been an official of US Military SouthCom previously, offered to help any way he could. He told Dr. Helkins that he had access to a dozen helicopters. Steve later wondered why we weren't able to make use of them in 2012.

My read: being there and saying you're going to be there are distinctly different.

Could be a metaphor for this entire journey.

•

Maritza Carbajal, who is always characterized as "Our Fixer," made it all work smoothly, translating and expediting. She's originally from Mexico, has spent years in the US and has done similar liaison and arranging for other documentary and television projects.

She and Spud reported on the meeting they had held the yesterday (Friday) in Tegucigalpa with the military—general, colonel, airport security, etc.—and our main man in Honduras, **Virgilio Paredes**, head of The IHAH.

We are now 100% melded with the government—apparently no NGO and our long-time ally/contact Cabinet Minister **Africo Madrid Hart** is not involved directly in our current process. The Hondurans have changed the way they are organized to deal with us frequently. Obviously, we have no control or input into their machinations. The government, including the military, are now our primary direct connection for the expedition. Our main thing is to develop and keep good relationships with them.

Spud and the others gave rave reviews to the Hondurans they had been with on Friday, "They were totally welcoming and cooperative on every level." It was apparent from the excellent vibes and how the whole Day-One process went without a hitch—except that Woody's personal baggage didn't show up from some other continent.

Remarkably, every other box and bag was there and efficiently loaded in vans to go to the Marriott in downtown Tegucigalpa.

All good at the **Marriott**. We got our rooms and keys in seconds from a special table in lobby that Maritza and Julie had arranged.

We all met an hour or so later in a conference room at the Marriot for a meeting conducted by Spud who introduced the colonel—smooth and totally businesslike. He had been on the Honduran President's special personal protection detail for years, looks like he's in his early 40's. It's unmistakable, this guy was in charge and was going to be a great asset for the duration of project—though some significant matters needed to be resolved, like where to land at **T1**, how the Honduran security forces would mesh with us, including how many and who's responsible for what, and especially how their helicopter which holds far more than ours would be deployed.

Unbelievable—all these anticipated events are actually happening.

And smoothly—so far.

#2 Onward To Catacamas
Sunday, February 15, 2015
Catacamas, Honduras

We left Tegucigalpa and set off to **Catacamas**. in an eight vehicle caravan. We arrived at our hotel in Catacamas by 4:30PM—less than five hours. Most of us were in a relatively comfortable airport-type van. The other vehicles included a truck with a fuel tank on the back for the first day of helicopter flights, a moving van with all the baggage, equipment, and stuff, a few military trucks with about 18 armed Honduran personnel, and an SUV with the colonel and his people. It all went smoothly across some scenic hilly and dry countryside.

We had planned to take a break in a small town along the way, but the colonel radioed our security crew that we should all pass right on through since it wasn't the time or place to stop. Some speculated about the reasons but nobody questioned the decision!

Lucian and Mark shot some intimate video inside the van, especially with Dr. Helkins who was wired and is the main on-camera through-line of the video so far.

We were also able to pull off a coordinated fly-by in the helicopter, and Josh went up and got

the footage of the caravan—his first helicopter experience ever. He was pumped and loved hanging out the side to get it all. "I only got sick a little when we shifted directions."

We got to Catacamas—it's the cowboy capital of **Olancho Department** with a population of 35,000—more than triple what it was in the 1970's. We put our personal and jungle-ready stuff in individual rooms of our HQ—the

Papabeto Hotel. Maritza had found it, checked it out in advance and made all arrangements. It all worked and is going to be safe—we do have armed guards 24/7—clean, and comfortable. It's exclusively ours for two weeks, even when we're doing jungle camping.

After a filling meal with kebobs, rice, guacamole and vegetables, we all went to a no-bullshit meeting at 5:30—about 25 of us including five Hondurans (the helicopter pilot, the colonel, two other military guys and Oscar Neil Cruz, the archaeologist from IHAH).

Woody conducted the meeting and said upfront that he wanted to listen to what everyone had to say, but the gravity of being safe and clear was primary and unmistakable. We then spent the next 90 minutes determining in no uncertain terms exactly what will happen tomorrow, Jungle Day One—who, what, where and when.

Bottom line is that we will do the reconnaissance in the morning, flying over our site **T1**—and maybe name it—in both our A-star helicopter and the Honduran military helicopter. Did I really write that last sentence? It's been 20+ years after our first inkling that this is the place and we'll be there in less than 12 hours! No matter what happens, it's the stuff of lifetime achievement and fascination. Imagine being in a location in 2015 that, as far as anyone can tell, hasn't been occupied or documented for 500 to 1,000 years.

•

OK, back to real: In the Airbus A-star, departing around 8 AM will be Lucian to shoot, Steve Elkins, Sully, the hazardous environment security specialist, plus a Honduran military guy. This is apparently an absolute requirement of the aviation authorities—nobody flies without a representative of the government/military. Seems to be a firm government regulation. Since our chopper has seats for four bodies plus Myles, our pilot, only those three from our group can make the first pass.

The Honduran military chopper (which seats 8 plus the pilot) will make the 30-minute flight in tandem carrying four military personnel along with Oscar, the archaeologist, Doug Preston and Dave Yoder who are under contract with *National Geographic* and not subject to the insurance requirements of UTL/Benenson Productions, and Juan Carlos Fernandez Diaz, LiDAR specialist from NCALM in Houston who is a Honduran national. Juan was with us for the scanning in 2012 and knows as much about the lay of the land in the site as anyone alive.

I think I have that right. If not, I'll send and update tomorrow.

The entire first foray should to take 30 minutes to get to **T1** and 30 minutes to get

back. Add in another 30 flying the length of the valley, ogling what's there and trying to determine a safe landing place as close as possible to our archaeological features. And, of course, figuring where to put the base camp—with some 15 tents and lots of gear.

Depending on what they find and how long it all takes, it's possible that we will be able to return later in the day to land and walk around a little. If not then, certainly we'd hope that happens on Tuesday. Woody has declared, "If we're not in the jungle by 2 PM Monday, we won't be in the jungle." Everyone is so hot to go—but safety and good judgment must prevail. Most likely we'll have a pretty full complement in the jungle by late Wednesday.

Also, depending on what's down there, it might require rappelling into the jungle to do the set-up and the first walkabout. Our British Special Forces guys have major experience in this. We also have another expert who just arrived today, **Daniel Navarro**, a world-class mountain climber and rappelling specialist. He's from Mexico, owns an equipment company and has been all over the world from the Himalayas to Peru and back. Daniel has been in some high places and has a delightful smile and laugh—he's another Maritza score. He gave a refresher course for those who plan to rappel if necessary. I skipped the session. I had enough trouble climbing the ropes in fifth grade.

During the meeting Sully was adamant about the dangers and the need to be completely together to use the rope to descend onto the jungle floor. "Rappelling is not a walk in the park," he warned. "It's only for those who have done it before."

•

We haven't left the Papabeto Hotel yet, but we did pass by the town square—maybe three square blocks with an absolutely gorgeous old ginkgo tree in the middle. The willowy landmark tree is likely a century old—but we're searching for something that's likely to have been around at least 1,000 years ago. Mind-blowing. As Steve said to everyone at the meeting, "When Chris and I get to the jungle, we're gonna plotz."

Exciting as all this is, there doesn't seem to be much fear in our group about bad outcomes—all the more reason to pay the strictest attention to the Special Forces guys and do exactly what needs to be done and no more. This adventure is not for the faint of heart or non-team member.

Tomorrow: looking for a major breakthrough on what's actually there.

Whatever it is, the world will find out about it real soon.

NOTE: When all this is over, **Chris Fisher**, our chief archaeologist, **Oscar Neal Cruz**, **Alicia Gonzales** and **Anna Cohen** have decided to jointly write an academic paper for submission to the **International Archaeology Association**. (See **Notes** for link.)

Oh, and a correction from yesterday: Steve says that U.S. Ambassador Nealon said he had sixty helicopters he could call on from South-Com—not a dozen as I had written.

#3 We Came, We Saw...
Monday night, February 16, 2015
Catacamas, Honduras

In some way this was one of the most successful days of our adventure for Steve and me. We have nearly two weeks—assuming the best—to do what comes next.

Yeah, we came, we saw, but we didn't conquer. "Conquer" became politically unacceptable here about 100 years ago, but foreigners—especially gringos—still wield major power.

We're more on a mission to understand, show, and explain why this little spot in a jungle—so far from our frame of reference or our era—matters.

There were cloudless blue skies for Flyover Monday. Fifteen or so of us went to the Catacamas airstrip in **El Aguacate** at around 8:30. Only our helicopter and the Honduran military helicopter and support personnel are at the "airport"—no other aircraft, no other people.

Today our helicopter worked, but the military's didn't. They had to come back after about 20 minutes in the air—a precautionary measure cuz some balancing computer wasn't doing what it was supposed to do to assure responsive flying. (Pardon all the technical jargon). Everybody came back and was perfectly fine.

So here's the deal—as Dr. Helkins says several times a day:
• Our little chopper, with Myles Elsing flying brilliantly all day, made three reconnaissance trips to look over the valley we first identified 18 years ago.
• Nine of us went to see the jungle target in three groups of three. Five more went in the replacement Honduran military chopper in the afternoon. Each trip was 30 minutes to reach the valley, another half hour or so exploring by air and then another 30 minutes back to Catacamas.

OK—as of tonight we know:
• The valley is right where we thought, a few miles long and a few miles wide.
• It's drop-dead gorgeous—a magical garden that emerges from dry land dotted with cattle grazing on ranches and countryside full of timber scars. We then see several miles of "broccoli"

from above—a thick impenetrable jungle.

And then suddenly there's a literally awesome spot that's protected by ridges on all sides, shaped like a kidney and with some visible flatter spots on the ground. We were just a few feet above it on some of Myles' dips down into the jungle.

• There's a river running through it that, at this time of year, is about as wide as a city side-street.

• Wow! We located a terrific and safe landing spot within 100 yards of our primary archaeological objective. **T1** is still the name we're using.

•

Interesting how perception and knowledge work. I saw nothing resembling "civilization"—no buildings, pyramids, or anything like that. Our archaeologists Chris Fisher, Oscar Neal Cruz and cultural anthropologist Alicia Gonzalez with their trained eyes, saw places they were certain contained evidence of civilization. We'll soon see. By the way, all of us could see layered formations that are probably places people lived centuries ago.

I'll spare you the rest of the details and process but, as a direct result of today's reconnaissance, we are ready to take the whole bunch of us into the jungle site tomorrow.

This will happen once our Special Forces guys clear a landing spot, cutting high grass and what looks to be banana tree leaves. Woody figures it should be less than two hours of sweaty work.

Next, they'll immediately go another 100 yards or so up a hill and set up our base camp, where 18 or so of us will live for the next 12 days, making video, archaeology, anthropology, and perhaps eventually, the history books.

Steve was thrilled today and for many reasons:
• Everything went smoothly and safely.

• He felt "vindicated" for all the years and thousands of hours he and we have spent imagining this place in the Mosquitia jungle, in the state of Olancho, in the country of Honduras—right where he and I thought there might be people living 1,000 years ago. 1,000 years ago!

• Our hoped-for ideal landing spot will work for us to maximize our efforts and set up a safe and strategic camp.

All of this was corroborated by Woody Wood who has been in more situations in more jungles than he can count. In fact, at the very moment Steve and Woody flew over the ridge several hundred feet above the spread-out hills, they and pilot Myles were in awe at how uniquely beautiful and special our little valley is.

To a person, the rest of us felt that magic too as we flew over the ridge and dipped deep down into the valley.

We have gobs of video footage from the day of flying, interviews and impressions before and after people flew and some remarkable pictures, including a set of stills that Dave Yoder was able to capture of the most striking and colorful birds I've ever seen—probably large blue and yellow macaws—that flew and swooped in groups of two to four.

But, let's face it, our primary interests are on the ground. Is it a lost city? Is it related to the legend of Ciudad Blanca? We'll likely have a good head start on it tomorrow, our first night in the jungle.

Within days, we'll know lots more.

At 5:30, we spent an hour or so at the hotel with Woody, Sully, and Spud helping get us prepared for the jungle with packs, boots, sleeping bags, canvas cots, Deet, sun screen, whistles, raingear, snake gaiters and water purifiers. They explained exactly what we needed to do with it all.

For the record, there was mucho discussion in an early evening meeting at the hotel with the colonel and his five men about the regulations and plans for tomorrow—who will go on the military helicopter, under what conditions and in what order.

One thing we now know is that the military personnel—now some 16 of them!—will camp a few hundred meters away from us near a different landing spot that is safer for their larger and less maneuverable chopper. If and when any of us goes with them, which we are now cleared to do, we'll be accompanied to our camp by the armed soldiers.

The bottom line is that the Hondurans are cooperating and doing the very best they can, given that they have to deal with us. We're visitors and foreigners who take pictures of every moment and every interaction. We have identified and are pursuing their cultural patrimony—and they need to be sure it stays theirs. We absolutely respect that and they respect our rights, both legal and scientific, to do what we were doing.

It was a complicated bilingual session. It mattered that we all get it exactly right. It turned out fine, reassuring each other that all of us—some 40 bodies total—were in this together and not as separate entities with our separate interests. Symbolically, it was shown by everyone passing around the sweet buttery carmel corn I had brought from Chicago. We were ALL-IN!

•

After the military left and we finished some dinner at the hotel, Woody delivered a detailed set of notes about the laws of the jungle for us, including:

• **Medical**—Drink water all the time, and if your urine is dark, you're not drinking enough. Accidents happen when people are tired and grouchy—that's when people fall, hurt themselves and create problems none of us needs. All three of the Special Forces guys are trained as medics and will help if we ask.

• **Wildlife**—We are not what they want to eat. Watch for scorpions, they can sting and cause real damage. Watch for snakes, especially the poisonous **fer-de-lance** which are around and prefer to come out in dark, but will only act defensively if they are stepped on or scared. So watch it! If any of us does get snake-bitten there is anti-venom serum ready to use and there will always be evacuation procedures in place 24/7.

• **Hygiene**—Wash every day and every night to avoid rashes, and skin problems. Wash whole body. Have three sets of fast-drying clothes, one to wear, one washed, and one drying. Woody reiterated that water is the key. We'll be eating dried or freeze-dried meals. He reviewed the toilet and rubbish procedures—as we've all learned, we'll take out everything we bring in.

• **Clothes for tomorrow**—boots, socks, long sleeves, sunscreen and Deet.

Some of us spoke. Chris Fisher made it clear that we ought not touch anything that looks like it could be a relic—it could be fragile. If and when we do find architecture that might have rooms, be totally gentle and don't touch.

Steve told us that we're all here for a reason and we have a truly unique and outstanding group. It's our absolute duty to take care of each other under all circumstances. He thanked us all for being part of this once-in-a-lifetime opportunity, including Bill Benenson, who's still in Santa Monica, for making it possible.

We thanked him for all he has done to make it happen.

All true—as is **The Lost City**, if you were to ask me.

We'll have two radio communications every day between Sully in the jungle and Maritza back at the hotel in Catacamas. If we need stuff or to communicate to the outside they'll make it happen.

In terms of my chronicles, you might not hear from me for a while. No cell tower in the Mosquitia! Be patient and don't worry. I will write, but I can't guarantee when you'll see it.

•

#4 Halfway To The Jungle...
Tuesday night, February 17, 2015
Catacamas, Honduras

I'm still in my room in the **Papabeto Hotel**.

Neither I nor eight others in our group were able to fly into the jungle base camp today. The fuel truck from Tegucigalpa that was scheduled to arrive at 8 AM didn't show up until 3 PM. We were on hold at the airstrip inside a 25x25 concrete hut.

Hot and quite a bit frustrating.

We did have enough fuel for two flights—plus holding the mandatory amount for an emergency round-trip—so the priority was to be sure that the three amazing Special Forces jungle guys got in early to clear out the landing zone for the rest of our comings and goings.

They finished that and went to work up the hill to set up the camp for the 16 or so of us who will spend the next 10 nights out there. The landing zone is a few hundred yards from the site of our most prominent area of archaeological interest. But, there is a steep hill to get to it and it's just about always raining.

Ace chopper pilot **Myles Elsing** did two Catacamas-jungle round-trips—about an hour each.

Around 11 AM word came from the Brits in the jungle via walkie-talkie or maybe satellite phone, that it was OK to land the first three of Our Gang—our director of photography **Lucian Read** from Brooklyn; lead archaeologist **Chris Fisher** from Colorado; and *NatGeo* still photographer **Dave Yoder**, originally from Indiana but for 30-odd years he has been on assignment on every continent. He's now based in Italy, an American citizen but not inclined to live there.

They all boarded the chopper, landed and haven't been heard from directly for about 12 hours. We do know they're in there and that if there had been any problems we'd know that too.

The next two to go were writer **Doug Preston** and image-engineer/mapper/pilot **Juan Carlos Fernandez**, a Honduran native who lives in Houston and works at the airborne LiDAR capital of the world, NCALM. **Chris Fisher** and Juan have been studying and manipulating the images we recorded in 2012 with **Steve Elkins** and occasionally with me, and have the definitive word on what features are where.

Chris, as a Latin American expert, will be a prime puzzle-solver about what is and was there, who might have been in this civilization, and how it relates to other sites and architecture in Meso-America.

Tomorrow, sound engineer and all-around joy **Mark Adams** and assistant camera and media wrangler **Josh Feezer,** from New York, will be first to go.

The third shift will be our analytic team, Honduran archaeologist **Oscar Cruz**, cultural anthropologist **Alicia Gonzalez** and archaeologist **Anna Cohen** from the University of Washington. The three of them spent many hours of our down day today talking and theorizing on what they saw in the fly-over yesterday and doing video interviews with our crew. They are two scientists who've been patient but eager to get past the starting line of ground-truthing at the site.

The last trip of the day will be our commander **Steve Elkins** and me, plus **Sparky Greene**, producer/jack-of-all-trades. In real life in Malibu, Sparky is a producer-writer-landowner and fitness/running freak. He and his wife Jill have a wedding venue business. Couples pay for the remote location, the facilities for catered events and especially beautiful Pacific views. Bill Benenson pays for and listens to Sparky's advice—they've both been around "the industry" for at least 25 years—so Sparky does his best to serve Bill's commercial and business interests, sometimes nearly impossible to assess. Sparky and I have become friends, but he's the kind of guy who almost always needs parentheses and a pre-excusing preamble before getting to the meat.

WHAT A TEAM! We came from all over the globe with widely varied experience and intertwined expertise. Age 22 to 70-something. We've been together 24/7 for four days. The trust, chemistry, strong ties and mutual respect continues to build. The inside-jokes and internal tales grow every day.

My take is that the bonds and interaction will continue to grow in the jungle. It's all unknown—seeing what's there, where it came from and how each of us will be able to contribute to the whole process. It's an adventure in so many ways.

•

#5 Archaeology: It's Like Picking Posies...
Late Thursday night, February 19, 2015
Deep in the jungle of La Mosquitia at T1, Honduras

... the only trick is you have to be in the right place at the right time.

And with the right people.

We have had a remarkable start. We discovered more than anyone could have hoped for in two days of searching this jungle. Thanks to the **LiDAR mapping** and years of studying the results, **Chris Fisher** and the archaeologists and the rest of us came to this dot in the vast jungle because we knew where to look.

This is a new kind of archaeology. It's genuine discovery, new ways of finding artifacts and evidence of civilizations. Then probing for answers about what to do with the findings and what they mean.

The first mind-blowing spot we found was about a 20-minute hike from our base camp, down the river and up a steep hillside.

Oh, and did I say it had been pouring for seven straight hours at the time which made for some serious sloshing around—especially for people like me who don't slosh much these days? At that first spot we discovered a cluster of obviously hand cut stones and steps.

The science and significance of our first breakthrough today will likely be described for years in popular media and academic journals. I'm not the guy to say much more than that, but for all 15 of us who experienced it first-hand, sharing that singular time and place, it is a ding-ding moment no one will never forget.

About three hours after we had left the camp, Steve, Chris, Juan and 7-8 others used a GPS with the LiDAR data embedded to track down a second spot we had planned to explore. They searched and found some interesting possibilities, but nothing certain.

While they were gone, Alicia, Anna, Sully and I began clearing the first location. Alicia and Anna wrote their notes and discussed that the artifacts were identifiable as part of a pattern that had shown up on the LiDAR and read as a large public space.

We marked off the location with yellow ribbons on trees. The second group returned and we had some hot tea with milk that Woody had conjured up to warm the innards of our soaked bodies.

Then we were a single unit on the move—a line of 15 muddy, rain-soaked and impossible to distract seekers of the unknown.

We had been trudging forward for 20 minutes or so when I heard a group of three or four about 15 yards back buzzing about something. They were ogling, shooting video and stills and speculating about a set of artifacts in the dirt. That brought on a different kind of chill than what the incessant rain had induced.

All of us surrounded the new-found relics. It was unquestionably what we had come to the jungle to see. Like the others, I had what amounted to an electric charge in my backbone. Chris Fisher loudly told everyone, "Whoa! Don't touch anything. Don't move anything." Oscar issued a warning in Spanish which Alicia translated.

The first sighting was made by videographer **Lucian Read** whose eyes were wide open as he was carrying his equipment. The experts were trying to assess the significance and roots of the symbolic sculpted pieces that were stuck in the ground.

There were dozens of them. The jaguar head—not a monkey as we first thought—was the most spectacular. But we also found metates—used as a grinding stone and ceremonial throne, broken stone vessels and other stone objects with hand-carved designs. Everything was a fragment. It seemed impossible that they had broken naturally or by accident. Why would they be sticking out in the mud in such a confined space? All that's for experts to study, probably for a long time. To me it was enough to be part of finding the amazing trove.

My thoughts went to the idea of discovery—how a place or a thing can lay where it has been for centuries, unseen and undocumented by humans until somebody comes along and relates it to the history and experiences of long-gone people. We didn't just randomly wander by. We were getting the first payoff, the first knowledge based on all the technology and decades of study and money that could be put together. I have to believe there are dozens more areas destined to be examined and documented with an overarching intent to preserve, protect, and carefully develop the cultural import of this patrimony of the people of modern Honduras.

That raises a multitude of questions as to whether to adhere to the traditional "proper" archaeological tenet of leaving it undisturbed in the location where it was found (in situ)- or finding a way get it out to scholars and the public to appreciate, raise money for preservation and have absolute tangible evidence of the find.

Tune in tomorrow—or next week when the decisions are made by the Honduran authorities. **Virgilio Paredes**, head of the IHAH, arrived this afternoon but didn't come out to the site.

•

So now we know... archaeology is NOT like bending down and picking posies.

It's much more complicated.

And fascinating.

And wet.

•

#6 We All Have Something To Do
Friday, February 20, 2015
Deep in the jungle of La Mosquitia at T1, Honduras

Here I am in the goddam jungle. Only Spud and Alicia are still here in camp at 11 a.m. The rest, including Virgilio, went on a hike to explore the section next to the site where we found all the artifacts.

I'm feeling like I have for most of my life—at camp and lots of other places—The Outsider who can't deal with his personals—actual physical possessions, aka "stuff"—or the missing elements inside my head.

Now, it's body parts too: big toe and bowels.

Then there's the frustrations caused by or exacerbated by sleeplessness:
• video incompetence
• mobility to go and do what others do
• losing stuff
• not having a spoon set aside for "meals"
• gagging on most of the freeze-dried food
• unable to create a dry place for my shoes and clothes.

Indelibly etched into my consciousness is a black and white print in my long-gone therapist's office:

"WE ALL HAVE SOMETHING TO DO."
-Nat Apter

I was up at 3 AM and wrote that last chronicle about archaeology as picking up posies. Tongue-in-cheek, but serious thoughts about LiDAR, finding places and things because you know where they are and then posing questions about what happens next.

Now, at 11 AM, I doubt I have much to add, yet I must have something to do as the rain has conquered our little world here more than ever.

•

OK, other issues, bigger questions?

Usually, the first things to check out are money and politics.

Where's the money?

For Hondurans, it's the value of the stuff. Nobody else can claim it.

They will protect it—like crown jewels.

Our potential value to them: money and power.

Everything we do will help promote the uniqueness. Our "one-off" documentation will result in increased public interest for Honduras and Hondurans. They will benefit from the newly created value and power.

And that can translate into money for us too. Our video is fascinating footage that corporate media will pay for.

The people and government of Honduras are positioned to benefit directly. Apparently the model of Africo's non-government foundation that was to have the ownership and management of the whole project along with the U.S. counterpart is NOT going to happen. The current president and head of the cabinet will be in charge of it all, keeping it in the hands of government.

How they did it with practically no resources is an interesting piece of the story. Virgilio has joined Steve (and Bill) in wanting to take some relics out of here to hype the whole thing in a more accessible place. If they want and can pull it off, they can do exhibitions and museum shows worldwide for big bucks, according to Doug Preston. And the money can help assure the continuation of research and development of tourist assets here in this unlikely spot on the planet.

Enough. Exhausted. I gotta try to sleep.

•

#7 Sorting It All Out
Early Saturday morning, February 21, 2015
T1, La Mosquitia, Honduras

I'm doing my best to keep track of the many threads after week one of our travels and the fifth night of the group's jungle activities.

For some, it's pushing on to explore more parts of the whole **T1** site that are identified as possible locations for new evidence.

Others are working at the prime site which is now called **Jaguar** after the most prominent carved stone work we found—since monkeys don't have ears on the top of their heads, we've agreed that it must be a cat.

A non-professional like me might call it the buried treasures of the Mosquitia. Thus far, it is the hot spot of the project.

The academics are still convinced that this is a place where many thousands lived some 800-1,000 years ago. They can't yet identify who those people were or how they might be related to other Meso-American civilizations.

Some answers could be forthcoming as new perspectives and leads are followed up every day. As usual, I have to say that I'm not the guy to even speculate on the archaeological or cultural significance. But I am certain that what's up that hill is something nobody has seen for a very, very long time. And, as we clean up around it, more features keep showing up. This is in the jungle mud. There is no way right now to tell what's underneath it, but there's a huge likelihood that we have literally found a key that will someday unlock knowledge and insight into the people of the long distant past. And that is amazing!

It's a place on this planet that remained unidentified until this week in 2015.

Everyone has been truly professional at the work they have been doing and it shows in the results thus far. The video documentation of every day's journeys continues intensely and quietly by **Lucian Read** and **Mark Adams** against massive and constant confrontations with this green and wet world. The media cards with all the video go back to Catacamas almost daily, weather permitting, via helicopter flights. They are being indexed and organized in the hotel by **Josh Feezer.**

Virgilio Paredes came out to the jungle and stayed for about 24 hours—enough time to become convinced that the science has paid off and that what we've found will have a major impact on Honduras and the rest of the world. He talked about scientific and historic value as well as the reality of its monetary value. Protecting this whole area and the artifacts is an immediate priority. He gets that.

Close to 20 Honduran military are now stationed at the site. How long they stay and with what orders is a discussion that has begun in earnest. Honduras needs to derive the benefits of its own patrimony. How to do that is a major concern for Virgilio and the entire government. Virgilio jumped on a late afternoon helicopter and Myles took him back to Catacamas. He plans to return next Wednesday with the Secretary of Defense and possibly other high ranking officials—maybe even the President.

•

Dave Yoder downloads hundreds of pictures every evening in the tent with the generator. He is a harsh critic of his work and though he hasn't shown any of it to Steve, me or anyone else—he calls us "the public"—it is absolutely clear that he is great at what he does, a true perfectionist and artist. *National Geographic* will have the

best possible images available here and they will have genuine value on an ongoing basis.

Early one evening, I sat down with Yoder for a cup. He had an Ace bandage wrapped around his wrist, between his thumb and index finger. "How do you take such amazing pictures with that bandage?" I asked. "First of all, it's on my left hand," he said. "Plus, you don't take pictures with your fingers. You take them with your eye and brain."

Meanwhile, we are awaiting the arrival of **Bill Benenson** from Catacamas where he landed yesterday afternoon. His reaction to the progress and the priorities he sets for the whole project with Steve and the rest of us will be a major factor in determining how we move forward in the next five or six days in the jungle—and, no doubt, for months and years to come.

•

#8 Success Already! (At Least A Good Start)
Early Sunday morning, February 22, 2015
T1, La Mosquitia, Honduras

We know now that we've found some part of what we have been after for nearly 20 years and what we think other gringos and locals have been tracking for at least 100 years before that.

So far we have seen and carefully not disturbed what archaeologist **Anna Cohen** has

inventoried—52 artifacts in one location with a footprint about the size of the pharmacy department in a Walgreens.

But we are just barely at the tip of what we can safely call a lost city (or possibly several).

What we have discovered is absolutely a discovery in the truest sense—finding something

133

nobody else has recorded. Discoveries in all disciplines follow the same pattern. In our case, it happened through a combination of leading-edge science and tools—from our start in 1994 to where we are today—with contributions from some of the smartest, most dedicated and hardest-working group of people I've ever experienced.

Plus leadership and vision by **Steve Elkins**— I doubt anything like this unprecedented process would have been possible without his determination, perseverance and knowledge based on unusual scientific and organizational skills.

•

I've buried one of the ledes. The chopper returned to the LZ yesterday with **Bill Benenson.** He is the one who believed enough in the possibility that this project would be important enough to have far-reaching effects on the planet and our understanding of it and human history. He was blown away when he trekked to the place where the artifacts had been found. Later, he found himself doing a stand-up piece on-camera at the site declaring his enthusiasm and understanding of the unique accomplishment.

•

All of this has been done amid massive mud and rains, personal discomfort even for the most experienced of us junglers, and five sightings of the deadly **fer-de-lance** snake were way too close for comfort.

But trudge on we do, with Juan Carlos and his ground LiDAR, Chris, Alicia and Anna with their experience to put it in context as Latin American archaeology scholar-practitioners, and the talented video guys, Lucian, Mark, and Josh, who have overcome enormous physical obstacles to accomplish world class documentation.

134

Left to Right: Woody Wood, ethnobiologist Mark Plotkin, writer/editor Tom Lutz (behind), Steve Elkins, Bill Benenson and Doug Preston

Add to this mix perfectionist *National Geographic* photographer Dave Yoder, who still hasn't shown any of his spectacular images, and Doug Preston whose on-the-ground broad knowledge, storytelling and some of the best question-asking ability I've ever known is inspiring for the whole group.

We all feel as safe as possible thanks to the three Brits, Woody, Spud and Stevie whose 24/7 support, guidance, discipline and experience allow us to do what we came for.

Dr. Helkins has called our outpost **"The Four Seasons of The Jungle."** Take it from me, you've never stayed at one quite like this!

At 5:30 this morning, **Oscar Neil Cruz**, the field-experienced Honduran archaeologist, woke up to pee and opened his tent flap with his head torch on. He saw the unmistakable triangular pattern on a **fer-de-lance** that he said was more than two meters long. It immediately reacted to the light and slithered away. We've been told (and seen for ourselves) that the animals are mostly oblivious to us—they have never seen humans and don't act defensively unless you step on them by accident. I didn't know anything about Oscar's incident until a couple hours later—probably just as well since his tent is about ten yards from mine!

So today is Sunday—we'll be out of here in

five days and there's no telling what else we'll find. What we have seen thus far is unarguably revolutionary—even for people like me who don't have any field archaeology experience it is amazing. Steve and I both feel it is already gratifying and justifying on many levels, after so many years of believing and not usually being believed. We'll save that for another chronicle and the documentary that will follow.

For the record, I'd say that what we've done so far isn't likely to be on a scale that will make a spectacular splash on the front page of the *New York Post* tonight. The pyramids, sacred gathering places, architecture, and icons are all buried in mud, under centuries of undisturbed dense forest growth.

Nothing we have found, like these **metates,** contradicts the locations shown in the images and information from our LiDAR data.

Small tips of objects that are poking up out of the ground just where they're "supposed" to be are indicators of lots of information to come. But it is already significant enough to force everyone to stop and reconsider—there was a significant and unknown population who civilized this untouched valley in the "bottle-neck in the Americas." They were able to import stones long distances and were adept at sculpting them with a unique style.

They were different from the Mayas and Aztecs in culture, art, architecture and many other ways.

When we leave, I'm positive that we'll have just a fraction of the answers—only a few good clues. It will take a long time to be certain about who they were, when and how they lived and why they disappeared.

#9 Found And Lost Again

Monday morning, February 23, 2015
T1, La Mosquitia, Honduras

Nobody questions that everything here is the patrimony of Honduras. Where it gets sticky is figuring out how this evidence of a culture that has been lost for a thousand years and the physical evidence that we found just this week can most effectively remain accessible for study, scientific exploration and, eventually, available for cultural examination—likely including tourism.

The first enemy is looters—people who take archaeological treasures for profit. We all know they exist.

This is also a documentation project. We've filmed dozens of hours with many more to come. It's also rooted in academic and scientific disciplines. Our long-range vision of the significance and protection are in total sync—how to deal with the details is an open and honest debate. And we are trying for resolution.

What will it take for our documentation to be successful in raising awareness and ultimately leading to responsible long-term use? How do the ethical and traditional archaeological principles conflict with the real politics of today? And because this has been a large-scale, highly visible project, are the security needs different from traditional archaeological efforts? How can the goal of promulgating the findings be implemented most responsibly? Is the idea of removing an actual object—a specimen—a valid way to raise money for future projects? And what's the best strategy for using this tip of the mountains of dirt we've discovered to meet our shared goals for the future?

Of course, the irony and reality is that the "we" in the equation isn't us—this group of dedicated interdisciplinary people who are putting forward our most sincere efforts to balance the documentation with the science— it's about Honduras.

And there's not just one Honduras. It includes a country, a government, national pride, a cultural heritage establishment, indigenous peoples, a unique ecosphere, financial interests and a military among many other things.

For centuries, it has also been a target for exploitation of its resources and its people— from both the outside and the inside. It is the original Banana Republic. Unlawfulness has been a deeply embedded characteristic in the culture for many years. That's the reality we now find ourselves trying to understand and deal with. Bribery and corruption are inextricable from the national operating system.

Virgilio Paredes left the site of the Jaguar/monkey/stairs/carved stonework convinced of the overwhelming value it can have for his country. He's not an academic archaeologist, but at this moment he has the responsibility to determine the policy and the fate of what happens after the rest of us leave La Mosquitia in less than a week. Last we heard, he wanted to have some tangible physical piece(s) removed and taken to the museum or Presidential Palace in Tegucigalpa, both as evidence and as a seed-builder for further development. He is also acutely aware of the danger and history of looting and destruction in his country. It's his priority to cut that off at the pass—perhaps by securing some objects and keeping armed military patrols here indefinitely.

·

Both **Chris Fisher** and **Anna Cohen** see this archaeological site as an integrated entity, a cache. Its significant value is rooted in its not having been disturbed for many hundreds of years. There are lifetimes of work and hundreds of physical and cultural levels to be explored and understood. To them, the removal of any piece or portion represents a compromise of the professional work that needs to be undertaken. The value of this discovery, they say, is to find it all in an undisturbed context.

·

Bill and Steve and about a dozen of the rest of us took part in a discussion under the tarp where we all eat. It was filmed for more than half an hour with two cameras.

Opinions on the shades of the grey future varied, but one possible solution was offered by **Alicia Gonzalez**—to try to locate and fly in Honduran archaeologist, **Gloria Lara-Pinto**, the widow of distinguished IHAH archaeologist **George Hasemann** and an expert on cultural patrimony. Her opinions on what to do and the dangers of looting could be relevant.

Our group may not come up with a united recommendation as we're coming from several areas of interest. But regardless of what we say, the final decisions are up to the Hondurans.

Virgilio has said that he will return to our camp on Wednesday and plans to bring the secretary of defense and the head of the cabinet, if not the president. It's a complex mix that perhaps has as many layers as the site itself.

The one thing we do know for sure is that when we leave, we'll have documentation of the archaeology, botany, cultural history and other scientific data. We'll also have the contemporaneous video interpretations and interactions of our distinguished group. These will have lasting value, no matter what happens at the site.

•

#10 The More Questions We Ask, The More Remain

Tuesday night, February 24, 2015
T1, La Mosquitia, Honduras

The incessant rain couldn't stop the investigating work on Tuesday. Two world renown ethno-botanists had arrived—**Mark Plotkin**, President of the **Amazon Conservation Team**, and **Luis Poveda**, Dean of Ethno-botany at the **University of Costa Rica** and the author of dozens of botanical and poetry books.

Today they walked up-river to a small waterfall, surveying the plant life and how it might relate to supporting ancient populations.

Their preliminary opinion from a few hours of travel is that there is no visible evidence of deliberate cultivation of what's called economic plants—papaya, avocado, and other

We don't know the dates or where these people came from or where they went. Mark Plotkin thinks that wherever they went and whatever caused their departure, it must have happened in a hurry—not unlike Pompeii. The fact that so many of the artifacts are broken might be an indication of the anger and destruction the inhabitants exercised before moving on. Doug Preston thinks this is a logical explanation.

•

This afternoon it was clear enough for two trips to another area of the site that we called **T3** three years ago from the LiDAR data. While in the same untouched valley, it is at least 20 miles away, far larger, flatter, and appears to contain more monumental structures than **T1** which we've been exploring for the last seven days. Pilot **Myles Elsing** said **Chris Fisher**, who has been seriously interested in T3 for two

edibles. That leads them to believe that it wasn't likely there was enough food to support a large population in this location. They were careful to say that it was only one day of observation so it is by no means conclusive. Studying stuff like that is what global advocates like **Conservation International** do all the time.

One unanswered question among the dozens that have been raised about this trip is how was it possible, without significant stores of agriculture and food, to have artisans capable of developing the skills and taking the time to create what we now know exists? Like so much of what we're dealing with, there are mountains of unknowns that encompass many disciplines—archaeology, culture, climate, ecology, etc. that need to be considered before we can understand what we're dealing with here.

years now, found some fascinating possibilities there. It's the location that LiDAR engineer **Michael Sartori** told us in 2012 was the most significant place to explore. He and I have a $50 bet pending—I got T1, he has T3, but we haven't vested judging power to anyone.

Bill, Steve, and **Juan Carlos** are all confident that there are relatively easy places to land our helicopter near the sites of interest. We hope to know lots more tomorrow if weather permits landing and checking out some of the featured T3 locations.

Myles also reports that Chris saw another square shape that looked to him like an exciting archaeological feature on the way back to our LZ, but outside T3.

We've been here for a week and had the opportunity to fly and walk all over the place, but we definitely have raised more questions with each set of answers.

Tom Lutz, author and founder/editor-in-chief of the *Los Angeles Review of Books*, spent three nights in the jungle with us and returned to Catacamas this afternoon. He's fascinated by what he has seen and impressed with the wide range of expertise in the group. He shares Doug Preston's opinion that the precedent-setting use of technology for finding sites that were never before visited is one key to what's important about this breakthrough archaeology project. As the author of ***Doing Nothing: A History of Loafers, Loungers, Slackers, and Bums in America***, he won the 2003 American Book Award—so I respect his perspective on me and our group of high-achievers.

The matter of what will happen to the site and the relics is a constant theme and a source of clearly differing opinions. I've written about this before and I will again.

The Hondurans have to decide. That could come as early as Wednesday when five government officials are scheduled to visit the site.

I have mostly written these pieces about what our remarkable group has done and is doing through the lens of the idea and impact side of our mission. For me, writing these chronicles reminds me of the days I was a sports reporter with an ongoing beat. It wasn't scholarly or science-based writing. Writing has always been fun to do and this is a payoff for all the incarnations of this chase Steve and I have been through since the mid-90's.

But in the jungle, the real work is detailed, down and dirty, and muddy—really muddy—each time it rains and this is not even supposed to be the rainy season. Even though it seemed like it was always raining in the rain forest, I was aware of some magic moments at night when we could see shooting stars through the trees and clouds. In fact, it happened often, always coming as a delightful surprise.

We are creating the video and audio elements for the documentary at the pace of about five hours each day. Actual treks to and around the sites are something on the order of another 4-5 hours daily, with us frequently divided into groups. Each trip includes Honduran soldiers who must accompany us on orders from the colonel, and each trip is led/managed by at least one of our three jungle experts. Our LiDAR data is united and preserved with maps and photos of the jungle using digital GPS equipment that I don't begin to understand.

After returning to base camp, the digital video cards are downloaded to drives for backup. It takes less than real-time, but at least an hour. Still photos for National Geographic are also downloaded to a drive. The field digital data goes into the archaeology computer database as do new ground-LiDAR images—its implementation is still in the experimental stage, or it was as of yesterday.

So this is all way beyond what many might have thought of as a bunch of adventurers in a tropical rain forest on treasure hunt searching for pieces of a lost city. We're doing a hard-core, state-of-the-art scientific and imaging journey, using sophisticated digital tools at every turn. And of course that requires us to have top people who can manage and use it to the fullest extent possible.

The results continue to be truly impressive.

•

#11 Slippery Slopes
Wednesday evening, February 25, 2015
Catacamas, Honduras

Our camp turned into a mud pit. Anywhere our team tried to go was slip-and-slide. But by the afternoon, it was sunny and beautiful.

Doug Preston, Bill, Steve, Mark Adams, and a few others went to "The Gap"—a spot about an hour's walk up-river that's the inlet to the valley. They report that it's a beautiful place and helps to explain how the people in the valley were well-protected as it seems to be the only way to enter.

Mark Plotkin said they had seen a stand of banana trees that must have been cultivated since they aren't native to the area. He also explained that it had to have been planted after Europeans entered these lands around 1500. So there's still no proof of ancient agriculture here. Why does it matter? If they could sustain themselves without hunting and gathering it would help explain how they were able to do the complex artistic work we know is here. But again, more questions. I haven't begun to grasp it or relate to it as spiritual or religious. We can barely ask those questions now, much less come up with reasonable answers.

Dave Yoder braved the elements and went for a late night trip to shoot some night-lit photos last night at the major cache of antiquities. I'm betting the photography is way-cool, but still, nobody has seen any of his pictures. Maybe that's what defines an "independent" contractor, but in Dave's case, control goes right along with talent.

Juan Carlos continued his mapping using the ground LiDAR. Chris trekked to a place that none of us had checked out. There were dozens more visible artifacts, though the big stuff is buried under mountains of earth.

The goal now is get everyone out of base camp on the helicopter and back here to Catacamas, where I arrived today. Myles made four or five 30 minute runs through the blue skies late in the afternoon, carrying three or four people at a time plus some of the equipment. So now it's down to five plus three Brits, Woody, Spud and Sully, who are breaking down the camp and trying to leave it as close as possible to the way they found it. (The TAFFS leader, Woody, has to move on to his next gig in Africa tomorrow.)

Chris Fisher is satisfied that he has done as much archaeology as possible within our time frame and is definitely ready to fly out today. All the others will also head out today weather and helicopter permitting.

It has been an unforgettable experience for all of us. We have several dozen hours of video that focus on what we did and what people think about it. Anyone who sees it will know how breathtakingly beautiful, insightful, and unique this place is.

The issue of what the Honduran officials will do is still front and center. Today is the day they are due to arrive here in Catacamas. None of us knows what they are planning, but Bill and Steve are ready to meet with them as soon as they're ready.

More on that another time. For now I'm out of the jungle, dry and with mudless laundry. Onward to el Norte.

#12 What Happened In The Jungle...

Saturday, February 28, 2015
Chicago, Illinois

... stays in the jungle! At least so far.

The government of Honduras is still saying it has no plans for excavating or removing any items from the site. Steve has stayed on in Tegucigalpa for meetings with Virgilio and others in the government. But we've learned that officials on all levels there are totally capable of 180-degree turnarounds without feeling any need to explain.

The next steps are to develop a plan with the Hondurans to let the world know about the significance of this area in the Mosquitia jungle both as an archaeological site and a unique environmental treasure, leading to cooperative ways to preserve it and protect it. That's a tall order but we can only hope that our trip, the knowledge we gleaned, and the documentation we produced will show the importance of this tiny but untouched natural and historic place.

Our mutual goal is to show the world that we all have the responsibility to magnify these efforts to build awareness worldwide of what humans have done, are doing, and must not do to our little planet. It will take major international cooperation and organizing to succeed but let's hope that we've provided a good start.

As for the actual physical location our group stayed in for almost two weeks—the camp, the paths, and the landing zone will all grow back and become part of what they had been for many hundreds of years—covered over and invisible. The new-found archaeological features probably do have the most value by remaining in situ until a full-scale effort can be made to determine all that can be found out about them. But, again, like **Jimmy Cannon**, "Nobody asked me."

Our exploring and documenting trip is over. We have all moved on to the next thing. I'm back in **Chicago**—from ninety degrees to nine in less than 20 hours.

In a few days, our full-scale all-encompassing expedition will be a memory—one that none of us will ever forget.

We all have the bug bites to remind us for a while. But the beauty of the pristine jungle, the unique and not-easily-explained relics we saw, and unprecedented group efforts to document it all will last our lifetimes.

Let's hope that, in human and personal terms, the education and resolve we all have will be spread to millions by the media we have created and the coverage of it.

It is likely to appear first in a *National Geographic* blog within the next week or two, followed by a preliminary recap by **Doug Preston**. The internet explosion and Doug's eventual "true story" book will keep it all going.

What a trip! It has been the experience of a lifetime.

•

PART FIVE: THE ADVENTURE OF A LIFETIME
...What Happened and What It Means to Me

The valley was 100% amazing, totally gorgeous, the very definition of unspoiled — almost spooky. Upon entering and almost all the time we were there, I couldn't stop wondering how it could possibly exist in the 21st century. Sure, it was a lost city, but maybe better experienced as a little lost magic dot on the face of the planet.

Being There

I'm not a poetry-memorizer and my classics and literary education is extremely limited compared to people who really learned it and could recite it.

But once in a great while, the words to songs I didn't even know I knew pop into and take over my brain. In my canvas chair, soaked 24/7 in that overgrown forest of huge trees, the words came:

"Once in a lifetime, there's one special moment, one wonderful moment when fate takes your hand. And this is the moment, my once in a lifetime when I can explore a new and exciting land..." *

It's kind of bizarre that our brains work like that: having **Anthony Newley** stowed away in my head in the jungle as I was drinking in the feelings of being in this mystical place. It was unlike anything I had ever felt – simultaneously eerie, exhilarating, and peaceful in a way that I would have thought impossible (assuming I had ever thought of it). And now it seems unlikely I'll ever experience it again.

But it was by no means an unmitigated personal success. I paid with my health.

There's some irony in the flip side of being absolutely out of my element – danger.

The threats were almost entirely out of my thoughts as I was sitting or standing alone, getting soaked just as the trees, ferns and ground mud were.

But, of course, I wasn't alone. About 20 men and two women were all within 30 paces. But I never heard them at all during those spaced-out moments.

The two women in our party, Alicia Gonzalez

* From *"Stop The World, I Want To Get Off"*
- lyrics by Anthony Newley / Leslie Bricusse.

and Anna Cohen, had their own area of the campsite, about 25 paces through the forest.

They had a simple gravity shower the Brits constructed for them. Their presence was important for the dynamics of the group. We weren't overwhelmingly macho guys, or overtly sexist, but if there was any tension it was mostly in the good-natured relationship between archaeologist Chris Fisher and his assistant, Anna. Alicia was a soft-spoken scholar and artist whose sloshing in the mud is not her longest suit. Aside from their scientific contributions, having both of them there helped reduce a "men-in-groups" mentality.

What's The Point

At my age, the object is to keep going, push hard and don't waste any precious time complaining, feeling sorry for yourself or permitting the inevitable physical deterioration to become the focus.

So I'm constantly aware of two close friends who were definite role models: **Studs Terkel**, a Pulitzer Prize-winning author and oral historian, and **Bill Veeck**, Baseball Hall of Fame owner, promoter and author. I spent hundreds of hours with each, producing television shows and videos with and about them in their last 30 years. They both said our public television documentaries were the best ever done about them. My goal was to portray their lives and vitality that continued until their final years—and of course, to hang out with them, soaking in some of their magic, frequently involving food and drinks.

Bill and Studs never stopped pushing or knew any way of being other than enjoying and bringing joy to others. The both affected

Studs Terkel (1912-2008) and **Bill Veeck** (1914-1986)

millions of others, who were influenced by their lives and appreciated their depth, intellect and humanness. They were loved and left wonderful legacies. They never shied away from and always accepted new challenges as long as they lived, except in rare instances when failing physical health slowed them down (but never for long).

So of course, I never considered compromise. I had to go into the jungle. This had been going on too long to cop out. I was compelled to relate well to all the others and to write about my experiences. If I hadn't, I wouldn't have felt alive and that, as Bill Veeck used to say, "is not a viable alternative at my age."

Both Studs and Bill were always loyal to old relationships and sought new ones every day, usually with younger people. They both got what they needed by knowing how to give others what they needed.

After they were "old," over 65, they followed **LeRoy "Satchel" Paige**'s philosophy, "Don't look back. Someone might be gaining on you." That says so much about living, competing, focusing, and persevering. No wonder he was the oldest player ever to play in Major League Baseball.

I heard Studs and Bill, both avid readers and writers quote **Mark Twain,** who said, "Age is a question of mind over matter. If you don't mind, it doesn't matter."

What DOES matter is how I felt about the experience, both at the time and now as I write this two years later. Finding the artifacts sticking out of the ground in the mud of a constant rain was a transformative moment of real discovery. It was unlike anything I ever felt before. It was spine-tingling! Here were these shards of pottery and artifacts that had been undisturbed for at least 500 years and we were the first people to find them. It was a good

high, in no small part because Steve and I had lived with the questions of where and what for almost 20 years. At that moment, on February 19, 2015, all that had led us to this point rushed into my head at once.

But I couldn't savor the rush up there on the hill with our group. Chris Fisher was shouting, "Don't move. Don't touch anything!" It took the conceptual and made it material. And we couldn't stay there. We had reached the end of our time on the ridge. We had to get back to safety before dark, to walk and slide down the slippery mud between the trees and get back to the stream. We had to cross it in order to return to camp before it got too swollen and impassable.

What's The Value of What We Found?

I've thought about that ever since that moment. On one level it was the joy, the accomplishment and the satisfaction of fulfilling the theories, scientific inquiry and pure hunches we had lived with since 1994. But the overriding value is cultural. The calculation of cultural patrimony took on a new order of magnitude as it became clear that it couldn't really be measured.

When people say, "It's not the money, it's the principle," the principle is getting a price put on it—a valuation. In this case, it can't be insured for any amount.

Sure, Bill Benenson and our project had spent close to $1 million to see and record all that we had done in 2012 and 2015. In 2017, my dear friend **Dee Davis** took the greater human value out of the equation and said, "You were speculators. House flippers. Pilgrims who put their money and telemetry and faith in the one true Monkey God." Acknowledging that there was money involved in the principle, Dee's point was, "You wanted to get your money back by

One of the 52 relics we found at T1.

being the guys who found what others couldn't."

That cache has incalculable value as the cultural patrimony of Honduras. And now it's in **Aguacate**, in museum cases under glass, in an attempt to bring the world to see the glories of the past Mosquitia culture. We were trying to find it and document it, but in the end we were the recipients of a gift from the Monkey God, for us to make it possible to pass it on in whatever ways it would survive in the future.

My Take

The 29 chronicles I wrote those nights in Honduras were more journalistic (telling what happened) than personal (how I felt about it). That's how I defined my role when we were there.

But now, as I finish these reflections two years later, I think of those experiences more connected to my feelings – like that unforgettable day we made the breathtaking discovery of 52 relics on the side of a hill; like how I felt the nights I couldn't sleep or eat; like feeling I didn't have the body strength to do anything, but had nowhere to go to be comfortable doing nothing; like being part of a marvelous group of 24

people, not one of whom was an asshole.

I'd had very little recent experience packing everything I'd need to survive for days in horrible conditions, or carrying it on my back to unknown locales. But that's what I did starting on Thursday, February 19, 2015, with a dozen or so other wanna-be explorers.

We walked across the river from our camp to the side of **T1** where we knew there something solid had showed up on the LiDAR. We got soaked to the gills in the unrelenting downpour, and sloshed through some muck that came up almost to my pupik (belly button).

Ramar of the Jungle, the TV show from when I was seven, flashed at the moment we got stuck in quickmud. But there was no choice but to keep trying to get up the slick hill, about 45 degrees in places, and slippery everywhere.

Behind me was **Sully Sullivan**, my strong Scottish support system who frequently

stopped my sliding and literally had my back, helping push me ever upward, or sometimes holding on to me and a tree.

After about 20 minutes of that struggle— it felt like hours—I made it to the level spot where everyone except Sully and I had already arrived. And that's when I caught up with our leader, Elkins, who had been challenged to get there almost as much as I was. My old and dear pal made the official announcement: "Yay! Old man Weinberg made it." I responded in song: "Yeah, I get by with a little help from my friends."

I knew for the whole time I was there that I didn't belong. And a case can be made that none of us belonged in that glorious spot in the jungle that Doug Preston called "More Jurassic than Jurassic Park." For sure, I didn't belong. I couldn't last as long as the others. The sleep deprivation, freeze-dried meals I couldn't digest and being totally soaked all the time had gotten to me. I had to get out of there before "the jungle lifers."

I had serious bowel cramps in the middle of my fourth night in the jungle. All I could think about was getting to the makeshift shitter, cross-laid trees with a stinking ten-foot hole underneath. It was about 25 yards from my campsite. My whole body was in pain – I really had to go. I think I put my snake gaiters on. I put my feet in my slippers and trudged through the mud as quickly as I could. I was in my jockey shorts carrying a dim flashlight, headed for the latrine.

Suddenly I heard Spud yelling at me, "Tom, what the hell are you doing? Where's your head lamp?" My small dim flashlight probably wouldn't have lit up a snake.

Spud had a lantern and went the rest of the way with me. It all worked out that night, but by the second morning after that, a day and night before any of the original party left, Woody and Steve and I all knew it was time for me to go back to Catacamas and the hotel. They could use my tent and campsite for new one-day arrivals.

With about ten minutes of prep time, I was on a helicopter back to Catacamas with almost all my stuff. Object permanence has eluded me for seven decades and when I was exhausted, mentally and physically, it was worse.

I was leaving the ancient civilization and going back to third world comfort: a hot shower, a bed, a roof and a real flushing toilet.

I did feel like a bit of a loser—I had been kicked off the island and the survivors made it through another day or two. But, I had gotten all I could possibly get. And given all I had to give.

After a few days, I felt major satisfaction knowing that together we had made the

discovery of those relics and the unknown civilization that was responsible for creating them. Nearly 20 years of chasing was justified. My feelings of inadequacy didn't last too long, but, I was physically in worse shape than I could have imagined.

We Had Reasons to Be Scared

Woody had been very explicit, warning us about the deadly **fer-de-lance** snake and how a bite from this jungle viper would put a person in a helicopter immediately, hopefully en route to a hospital for life-saving anti-venom.

We did have some anti-venom to inject that Maritza had scored from Mexico. That snake was the obvious #1 threat. It kills more people than any snake in the Americas.

And they did show up for us – five of them in our camp in eight days. The first one, Woody had to kill because it didn't seem to have any inclination to leave the camp. The others slithered away.

There was other stuff to worry about—the bugs, the mosquitoes, spiders, monkeys, and God-knows-what within close range but not easy to spot. Some of our people saw jaguars.

The Sandfly and Leishmaniasis

Ironically, the one creature that wound up doing the most damage was just about the smallest – the sand fly.

Leishmaniasis wasn't on my radar until I got it in 2015. It was barely mentioned as one of the possible jungle dangers. The snakes, spiders, mosquitoes, cats, and monkey business attracted more of our attention than the barely-see-um sand flies—a small percentage of which carry a parasite they've picked up by biting a dead mammal or other decaying animal. Its little bite can give you big

skin lesions that can last many years, perhaps the rest of your life.

Within two months of our return a number of people in our group started to experience symptoms that were eventually identified as Leishmaniasis. At least five doctors in Chicago told me they hadn't heard anything about it since med school. And had never seen it. They would have if they were treating vets or patients in Afghanistan, Iraq, or if they practiced in Sudan, Bangladesh, Brazil, or India.

We became the experts in cutaneous leishmaniasis in 2015. Ten of our core group got it. At least ten of the Honduran military guys who were with us at all times were also afflicted. Steve Elkins and Bill Benenson managed to escape it. Five of our group were able to heal their lesions and kill off their parasite after a week or ten days of four-hour infusions of

strong medicine – kind of like chemo – at the **National Institutes of Health** in Bethesda, MD. They set up a research project for our group since we had all been in the same place and our disease could be studied, perhaps leading at some point to a vaccine. Just about everyone had side effects from the infusion treatment – stomach problems, kidney overload, fatigue and weakness, headaches, etc.

I might be getting a little ahead of myself, but now, two years after the jungle, every one of us still has visible evidence of our lesions. Fortunately, that thing on our skin was the only lasting symptom. Leishmaniasis has a small —less than 5%—possibility of spreading from the skin (cutaneous) to the nose and head (mucosal) or to internal organs like the liver and kidneys. When it's mucosal, it can literally eat

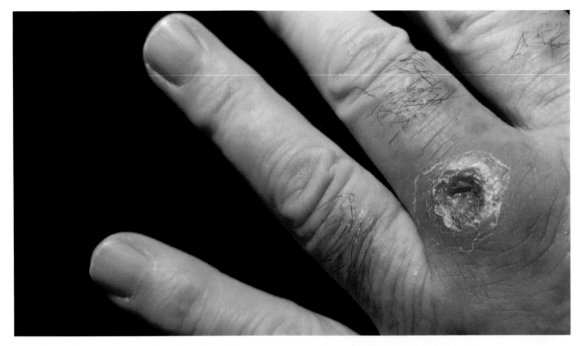

my face that drained my energy big time. That was followed in a couple weeks by what came to be diagnosed as cellulitis, (though the docs had called it a reaction to antibiotics) for about a week. I wound up in the emergency room and had to spend two nights in hospital before insisting on going home, against some medical advice.

Within a couple weeks, I was almost back to normal strength when I got a scare because my whole body was covered with measles-like spots and I had to sleep about twice as much as I usually do – ten or 11 hours instead of five or six. I was diagnosed with a particular strain of **vasculitis**, called HSP, which is most prevalent in kids.

It took about two more weeks to feel about 80%, when one more set of bacteria found me – a strep infection. More antibiotics and ten quiet days later I was ready to start the cure for the Leish parasites.

the skin off your face and be lethal, so it's a real good idea to try to get rid of the parasite when it's only in a spot or two on the skin.

My only lesion is on the knuckle of the middle finger of my left hand. In May 2015, I went to the NIH to consult with **Dr. Ted Nash**, who had been supervising cases for our whole group. After about 45 minutes of exam and discussion of options, we agreed that I could get comparable treatment in Chicago at the highly-rated **Rush University Hospital** in its infectious diseases unit. It's about 15 blocks from my home and much more appealing than staying in Washington, DC, for more than a week of debilitating 3-5 hour treatments.

After the jungle and before the infusions, I was beset with one problem after another. Within weeks of when I got back to my life in Chicago from the jungle, I got a bad staph infection on

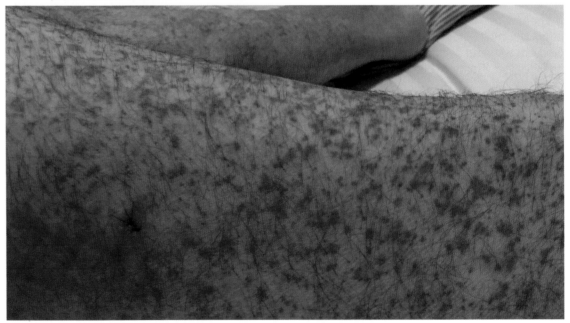

Mine took longer than most of the other guys' treatments because my old kidneys didn't like processing the possibly poisonous medicine—**Amphotercin**, sometimes referred to as "Ampho-terrible."

I give huge thanks to **Dr. Kamaljit Singh**, a global infectious disease doc, who was able to unravel the symptoms and solve the puzzle of my overlapping problems. He is a genuine healer and we became close friends. He helped me get free of the parasite, at least for a while.

Like the other patients in our group, I came out of the treatments without having the Leish spread. We all survived the infusions. Several, like me, had relapses in which the lesions reappeared and needed a new round of therapeutic treatment. This time it was a capsule I took for 28 days. This **miltefosine** was approved for clinical use in 2016. The supply is extremely limited and the (retail) cost is said to be about $700 per pill. I took two per day for a month. Do the math. Thankfully, we the taxpayers paid for it through the experimental project at NIH.

The damn infected sand flies kept me handcuffed for nearly two years. And it's possible that my immune system was compromised.

I never ran a marathon, did a triathlon or played the violin, before or after the jungle, but as I write this in 2017, I'm just about physically even with my baseline before I ever met a sand fly.

•

What About The Documentary?

As I look back at all that I've written in these pages, I realize that I haven't placed much emphasis about the documentary video images we recorded. Just about every day of my life I have focused on TV and video from the moment our family got the first television set in the neighborhood in 1947. I have spent literally thousands of hours conceiving, writing, recording, editing, broadcasting, archiving and teaching documentary/non- fiction TV and video for nearly 50 years. I've easily made it to the **Malcolm Gladwell** 10,000 hours that qualifies me as an **Outlier**.

My feelings about the documentary started to become clear in 2013 after **Doug Preston**'s long piece in *The New Yorker*. It was the foundation for the global perception of what we had accomplished as it filtered through the media around the world. And it had no less impact on our own heads and what would follow.

Up until the article was published, I still thought the "explosion," as **Bill Benenson** had wisely articulated it back in Roatan, would be told from the perspective of the documentary we were producing. It would be an emotional story about what we had done—innovating and discovering with LiDAR and—even more significantly—what we actually found and did in the jungle after a search of more than 20 years.

In his article, Doug was wonderful with the history of legend of the legend of the Lost City, our search and the significance of the LiDAR. The focus was primarily tracing Steve Elkins' process to make the project happen—though the anecdotes about **Bruce** and **Mabel Heinicke** were the most colorful.

But, as published, the article made no men-

tion of our plans to produce a documentary that traced the roots of the legend, our involvement from the start, and our plans to go into the jungle to "ground truth" what we'd found with the LiDAR. Bill Benenson was mentioned only as a source for funding the LiDAR mission. I wasn't mentioned at all.

At first I felt slightly slighted. Then I realized that MY personal vision isn't what mattered. The science and archaeology were the context for our whole project. But, WE were the players on the field, the participants. Our focus was on documenting it for all time on video and film. I felt that focus hadn't been communicated well enough.

It has taken a while to understand and realize how much it's not about me. I don't need to put myself into the limelight. My satisfaction with our discovery was in being an influencer all through the process. I admit there was, and maybe still is, a tinge in my psyche that felt **Dangerfieldian**—just got no respect. But that's not new. Over 50 years of working on collaborative projects that I thought mattered, I've always felt it was right and productive for others to get the credit they deserved.

One of my skills is to find ways for people to feel good about what we're doing together. That's not a *hard skill* like using the portable and digitally-loaded LiDAR equipment the way **Chris Fisher** and **Juan Carlos** were able to do, or getting world-class audio like **Mark Adams**. I'm not the coach. I'm not the quarterback. But I know that the results would be noticeably worse if I didn't contribute my part. And that's fine with me.

The disappointing reality is that more than two years later our moving pictures have yet to be seen, although dozens of the pictures in this book originated as frames from our video

Mark Adams and Lucian Read in the river below T1.

footage. That's not about me personally or not getting the public recognition. It's because my vision and excitement about our mission hasn't been articulated in the way or in the time frame that I'd hoped for.

This book helps put my part of the story in its own context. I know that what we wound up accomplishing was remarkable. None of it would have happened the way it did without Bill Benenson. But without a documentary reflecting my sensibilities, this book represents my point of view as well as I can express it.

Bill has been working on producing a documentary film—or possibly a multi-episode TV series—preliminarily titled *Curse of The Monkey God*. I know it will be powerful and stunning. As co-producer, I've screened dozens of segments and rough edits. I have provided notes and contributed to the process, but my vision of telling the inside story, spiced with informal and revealing spontaneous moments beyond the process of exploring and talking directly to the camera will never be part of it.

So I feel lucky to have this book reflect my personal experiences and feelings. My vision is now in words and still pictures, a new, challenging and significant way—at least for me—to express my perspectives on 20-plus years on the project.

•

The Aftermath

The Hondurans Took Over

When we left the jungle, the Hondurans took active control of the archaeological efforts. It became a permanent base for about 25 soldiers to protect the site. They committed to ongoing jungle maneuvers and training. I was reminded of what Sully told me while we were debating whether to leave the relics in situ or move them out.

"It was a case of the fox guarding the hen house," Sully said. "I've been a soldier for more than 30 years and I know the mentality. If there's something to guard, some of it always disappears." But, there wasn't much choice—it did belong to Honduras and that was the best way for them to try to protect it. As far as I know, nothing is "missing."

In January of 2016, a new archaeological expedition was put together by the **IHAH**. **Chris Fisher**, **Anna Cohen** and Juan Carlos Fernandez Diaz from our group joined them for a month-long project. (**Oscar Cruz** hadn't recovered fully from the Leish and didn't return.) They found more than 500 relics—or parts of them—at or near **T1**. They brought them out to a newly-constructed museum near **Catacamas** at **Aguacate**, the makeshift airport we used as the base for our helicopters. It was originaly built in the 1970s by the CIA for staging the Contra intervention into nearby Nicaragua.

Ciudad Blanca got the full public relations treatment. President **Juan Orlando Hernandez** went there to declare the tourist developments of the Mosquitia region. **Steve Elkins** and **Virgilio Paredes** joined in the press coverage, singing the praises of the possibilities for this area to be saved from further deforestation and evolving into a money-making venture for Honduras.

A French company paid the government and created a package of slick graphics and a multi-part TV series. The new name given to the area was *Kaha Kamasa*, derived from a Miskito language name for Ciudad Blanca. The stories and hype online and in print seemed like they never stopped. The Hondurans took full advantage of social media, particularly Facebook.

The government issued postage stamps to commemorate the discovery and the future tourist destination.

Steve Elkins; Honduran President **Juan Orlando Hernández; Chris Fisher;** and **Ramon Espinoza**, Minister of Science and Technology at **T1** in January 2016.

160

Our Public Presence

Our group was on the awareness-building circuit throughout 2016. Steve did gigs that included a trial lawyers meeting in Hawaii, the Explorers' Clubs on both coasts, and he spoke to a distinguished group in the auditorium at **Cedars Sinai Hospital** in Los Angeles with a crowd in excess of 100. It concluded with a generous free buffet after the free lecture. **Sparky Greene** and several of our group were there. Steve wowed them with detailed and vivid stories of our entire adventure.

In January 2017, **Doug Preston** did a book tour across the country. He filled a large auditorium at the **American Museum of Natural History** in New York, telling how when he worked there fresh out of Pomona, writing/editing the newsletter, he sneaked in late at night with a pal. It sounded like the original real-life *Night at the Museum*. He hung out just about all night with **Lincoln Child** with whom he later co-wrote two dozen thrillers and sold sixteen trillion books. His talk at the Museum was totally sold out with over 300 people and lots were turned away.

Doug did his best storytelling—self-deprecating, ironic and captivating. Hachette/Grand Central sold and Doug personally signed close to 200 books, more than half of which had already been bought with the $50 ticket. One book that the buyer asked both Steve and me to also sign sold for $125 on e-Bay a couple of weeks later.

With all the advance sales and promotion, *The Lost City of the Monkey God* hit the *New York Times* bestseller list the week it was released and stayed there for five consecutive weeks—a hit, but not quite the smash that Doug had hoped for. He's still optimistic about

American Museum of Natural History, New York - Weinberg, Elkins and Preston.

the sales of the paperback.

Chris Fisher did some 10-minute segments on *All Things Considered* and **NPR** at least twice. He was one of the most oft-quoted scientists for months in dozens of online and print outlets, from *Science Magazine* to the London trash-talkers.

Juan Carlos, Chris, Anna Cohen, Oscar Neil Cruz and NCALM Director **Ramesh Shrestha** delivered a scholarly paper to the **Academy of American Archaeology** in Mexico and co-wrote an important piece in its peer-reviewed journal for **PLOS—The Public Library of Science**. (See **Notes** for Link.)

Dave Yoder's pictures were in a thousand online and print articles—worth at least a thousand words for an already world class photographer.

I talked to a few reporters in Chicago and Madison on the phone, but mostly I was a full-time patient and video archivist, getting infusions and struggling to make it up to my third-floor Greektown apartment with two bags of groceries.

I did love one gig I did. The venue was the social studies room at **Braeside Elementary School** in Highland Park. Both fifth grades sat around for about 80 minutes with me after their lunch, talking about the pictures I showed them and asking lots of questions.

The snakes and the monkeys were their favorites. For the occasion, I invented *My 12 Steps to Discovery* reflecting what I had learned in the past 20 years. (See **Notes.**) My grandson **Lucas Prout**, a genuinely budding animal scientist, was at the front table, beaming about how cool his Gamp was. It made my Spring.

In spring 2017, **Conservation International** sent twelve scientists—mostly Honduran experts—to T1. This **"Ecological SWAT Team"** reported some "remarkable findings." They documented a snake previously believed extinct in Honduras since a single individual was discovered in 1965, a worm salamander with an implausibly long tail, several butterfly, amphibian and bat species that have never been found before in Honduras and the longest beetle in the world—the "Hercules Beetle." They also had a close-up encounter with a rare and scary puma.

The experts reported that the richness of species was overwhelming—indicative of the large area of unexplored, intact forest in the Mosquitia. This is only the first of many possible discoveries, if the area isn't messed up by modern interventions.

Government Intrigue

The foreign intrigue never stopped in Honduras. Despite talking about entering the private sector and/or moving from Honduras, **Virgilio Paredes Trapero** was still at the helm of **IHAH** into the summerr of 2017. He traveled around the world discussing museum deals for the artifacts.

Africo Madrid Hart was a curious case. He was our guy in charge, "the governor" of the Lost City of Ciudad Blanca from the start at the Miracle Meeting at the church with Mabel in 2009. He and his family became good pals with Steve, in contact almost daily for a couple years. His strategy for the project was to establish and operate an NGO to keep the Honduran Government out of it because

a) they couldn't move fast enough, and

b) new guys come into power all the time. True, they were all from the same couple dozen families, but there was constant scramble for who was on top at any given time.

We were involved long enough to experience that after less than five years later, the Hernandez government stayed in power. Africo and ex-prez Lobo became outsiders. Africo's rival within the party, Hernandez, held tight control of his government and the military.

•

An Amazing Adventure

This entire adventure was beyond any documentary I've ever been involved with. It was more about experiencing every moment than documenting them. Eventually the documentary will tell some of our stories as only video can. But the Lost City experience has been something almost totally different for me. Documenting it mattered, but this was never just another documentary to add to my list of hundreds of producing credits.

It was the personal adventure of a lifetime —with major impact on my mind and body— unprecedented and indelible.

It brought out the best of my abilities and my most vulnerable feelings.

I have confidence in myself. I have always made things happen that didn't exist before. That's why I've been called "creative" for most of my life. But I also carry around the flip side: doubt. Even the lost city discovery is filtered through my uncertainties about being real and not a fraud. Did we make such a big deal about it that we could and did fool everyone, including ourselves? Were those signs of life that we found as unique and important as we thought or were they "just the same old stuff in the jungle?"

How much lasting impact would what we did and found have on people's understanding of our world and history? Did it get more real the more we talked, wrote and documented it on video? Was my involvement real, or was I just physically present? (See **Notes** for Elkins' answers.)

Realistically, that was all in my head. I'm sure the feeling that "It's all a fraud" isn't unique to me. This time though, we asserted —albeit responsibly and carefully—that this was genuinely important. Virgilio called it "The most important discovery of the century."

I've always been on the lookout for hype. Now, was I part of perpetuating it? Mostly, I let go of this, but I guess a small part of me takes the expression "There's always room for doubt" literally.

What Do You Do?

"Have you retired?"

All of us greybeards get asked as many times as we're out and about.

For 30 or 40 years, I've said, "I'm a TV producer."

That usually satisfies them. After returning from the jungle, I felt like responding, "I'm a full-time patient," inspired by **Abbie Hoffman**'s sworn testimony as a defendant in the seven-month long 1969-70 Chicago Conspiracy Trial.

[U.S. Attorney: "And what is your current occupation, Mr. Hoffman?"

Brilliant Abbie—who had been a Freedom Rider in Mississippi, a radical street organizer in New York, a psychologist and mental hospital worker with two graduate degrees and author of a dozen or so books—replied:

"Right now, I'm a full-time defendant."]

He got a good laugh then, but only since the Mosquitia do I fully comprehend the ironic wisdom.

•

Would I Do It Again?

That's the question I'm asked more than any other. And I never hesitate to say, "Yes."

It's impossible for me to imagine not playing it out and satisfying my 20 years of chasing. I never would have predicted the health struggles I've been through but I've never looked back with regrets.

First, it was the logical fulfillment of the vision and hopes that Steve and I had for all that time, when nearly everyone thought we were goofy.

Second, the experience of being there is one of the things that has made my life worth living. I'll carry the overwhelming beauty and magical feelings with me for as long as I live.

I never have and never will do what we did as a group, a unit of intense, focused and achieving characters for whom nothing existed outside that jungle.

The idea of influencing how history is interpreted is a genuine accomplishment, even if it's only looking through a relatively small and specialized lens.

Yeah, I'd do it again, but I have no desire to go back! I guess I could say, "I already gave at the jungle!"

•

ACKNOWLEDGEMENTS

Elan Soltes, without whom it wouldn't be the book it is. Or probably even a book at all. His extraordinary artistry is evident on every page.

My involvement began with **Steve Elkins**, long-time friend, collaborator and inspiration for never giving up. **Janet** and Steve's generosity made it possible for me to work and live comfortably for dozens of stretches in Southern California.

Bill Benenson and **UTL/Benenson Productions** made the entire Honduras adventure and discovery possible. They also generously gave me permission to use frames from the documentary and the masterful images by **Roberto Ysias**. Without them, there would have been very few pictures.

Doug Preston, a model for what a writer and decent human being can be. His encouragement to create a picture book companion to his best-seller was the underpinning for this book. Also, without his providing unique photographs, this book would have been incomplete.

Terry Dawson was key to the successful process of creating stills from dozens of hours of video. **Wendi Weger**, COO of Benenson Productions helped all the way.

I'm grateful for months of editorial and conceptual contributions from **Nancy DeFrance**, **Sparky Greene**, **Eleanor Bingham Miller**, and **Andrew Seeder**.

With the advice and good counsel of **Matt** and **Ronnie Balson** and **Larry Kirshbaum**, I was able to keep the publishing of the book on track .

Dave Stern and **Rick Kaempfer** of Eckhartz Press have been 100% positive and helpful from our first meeting.

I must include Sally Station, who has saved my butt at the last-minute in dozens of projects since the 1970s.

Plus many others who've helped unselfishly on the long path of concept to publishing,including: **Eddie Becker, Sara Chapman, Len Elkun, Robert Feder, Chris Fisher, Thea Flaum and Bob Hill, Alicia Gonzalez, Anna and Kicker Kliner, Rick Kogan, Eric Kramer, Donna Blue Lachman, Todd and Brian Musburger, Steve Morgan, Virgilio Paredes, Russell Porter, Kamal Singh, Carol Weinberg** and **Jesse & Diane Weinberg**.

Finally, I must acknowledge **Bruce Heinicke**, a remarkable character and a guy none of us who were involved will ever forget. RIP.

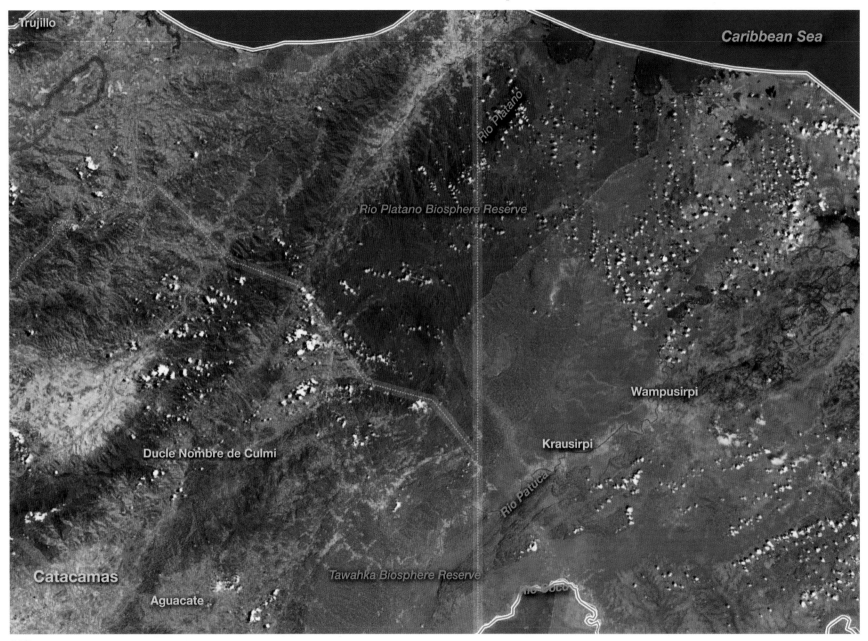

Links To Online Sources

Doug Preston's stories for *The New Yorker*:

- *The Lost City*, October 20, 1997.
  http://www.newyorker.com/magazine/1997/10/20/the-lost-city

- *The El Dorado Machine*, May 6, 2013.
  http://www.newyorker.com/magazine/2013/05/06/the-el-dorado-machine

- *An Ancient City Emerges in a Remote Rain Forest*, January 1, 2017.
  http://www.newyorker.com/tech/elements/an-ancient-city-emerges-in-a-remote-rain-forest

Doug's stories for *National Geographic*:

- *Exclusive: Lost City Discovered in the Honduran Rain Forest*, March 2, 2015.
  http://news.nationalgeographic.com/2015/03/150302-honduras-lost-city-monkey-god-maya-ancient-archaeology

- *Lure of The Lost City*, National Geographic Magazine, October 2015.
  http://ngm.nationalgeographic.com/2015/10/lost-city/preston-text

- *Excavation of Ancient Lost City Yields New Finds*, January 13, 2016.
  http://news.nationalgeographic.com/2016/01/160113-honduran-lost-city-archaeology

- *See New Discoveries at the Mysterious City of the Jaguar*, February 9, 2016.
  http://news.nationalgeographic.com/2016/01/160112-honduras-lost-city-archaeology

Doug's story for *Foreign Policy Magazine*:

- *The Design and Fall of Civilizations*, December 9, 2013.
  http://foreignpolicy.com/2013/12/09/the-design-and-fall-of-civilizations

Other *National Geographic* stories:

- *Newly Found "Lost City" Protected by Honduran President*, March 15, 2015.
  http://news.nationalgeographic.com/2015/03/150313-lost-city-honduras-protected-conservation-archaeology

- *Explorer: Legend of The Monkey God*, National Geographic Channel, October 3, 2015.
  http://channel.nationalgeographic.com/explorer/videos/the-long-lost-white-city

- *Pernicious Parasite Strikes Explorers of "Lost City"*, October 19, 2015.
  http://news.nationalgeographic.com/2015/10/151019-leishmaniasis-lost-city-Honduras-Mosquitia-parasitic-disease

- *Seven Major Archaeological Discoveries of 2015*, December 28, 2015.
  http://news.nationalgeographic.com/2015/12/151228-top-archaeology-discoveries-2015-naledi-Tut-treasure-lost-city-Nefertiti-Jamestown-San-Jose

- *Archaeologists Begin Excavation of Honduran "Lost City"*, January 12, 2016.
  http://news.nationalgeographic.com/2016/01/160112-honduras-lost-city-archaeology

Link to the dozens of press reports and reactions to the news of our LiDAR discovery in May 2013.
https://www.bing.com/news/search?q=lost+city%2c+honduras%2c+2013&FORM=HDRSC6

Chris Fisher's expedition notes for *Legacies of Resilience*:

- *Media FAQ for the UTL Mosquitia, Honduras project 2015*, March 8, 2015.
  http://resilientworld.com/2015/03/18/media-faq-for-the-utl-mosquitia-honduras-project-2015

The Public Library of Science (PLOS):

Research article by Chris Fisher, Juan Carlos Fernández-Diaz, Anna S. Cohen, Oscar Neil Cruz, Alicia M. Gonzáles, Stephen J. Leisz, Florencia Pezzutti, Ramesh Shrestha, William Carter:

- *Identifying Ancient Settlement Patterns through LiDAR in the Mosquitia Region of Honduras*, August 25, 2016.
  http://journals.plos.org/plosone/article?id=10.1371/journal.pone.0159890

CBS Sunday Morning:

- *Search for A Lost City*, January 8, 2017.
  http://www.cbs.com/shows/person_of_interest/video/bAY37hURxmqILQJEanOibVqSa5Dv78lh/search-for-a-lost-city

E-Mail From Steve Elkins - 12 October 1994

TO: TOM WEINBERG

FROM: STEVE ELKINS

DATE: 10/12/94

REF: CIUDAD BLANCA

THE LOST WHITE CITY EXPEDITION COULD OCCUR EITHER IN EARLY SPRING 95 OR JANUARY OF 96. THE ACTUAL EXPEDITION WILL LAST 4-6 WEEKS. THE EXPEDITION TEAM MUST TRAVERSE EXTREMELY DIFFICULT JUNGLE AND MOUNTAIN TERRAIN. TRAVEL WILL BE BY CANOE (OR SUITABLE INFLATABLES, AND FOOT. IT MAY BE POSSIBLE TO ARRANGE FOR SOME HELICOPTER SUPPORT (ITS DANGEROUS AND EXPENSIVE).

COMMUNICATIONS CAN BE VIA SATELLITE PHONE AND/OR VIDEO SATELLITE LINK. IT SHOULD THEORETICALLY BE POSSIBLE TO ARRANGE 2-WAY VIDEO COMMUNICATIONS WITH A BROADCASTER. THE SATELLITE PHONE WORKED IN MOST LOCATIONS ON THE EXPEDITIONS OF WINTER 94. I WOULD ASSUME A VIDEO LINK WOULD WORK AS WELL....ESPECIALLY SINCE THEY ARE QUITE PORTABLE THESE DAYS. ALL OF THIS COULD ALLOW FOR LIVE PROGRESS REPORTS OR INTERACTIVITY WITH AN AUDIENCE.

I ESTIMATE COSTS FOR THIS EXPEDITION TO RUN BETWEEN $350.000 AND $500.000. IT DEPENDS ON WHETHER AIR SUPPORT AND VIDEO SATELLITE COMMUNICATIONS ARE USED. THESE COSTS INCLUDE THE COST OF MAKING A TV SPECIAL AND THE ACTUAL EXPEDITION.

THE EXPEDITION WILL OCCUR WITH THE ASSISTANCE OF THE HONDURAN GOVERNMENT AND THE INSTITUTE OF ARCHAEOLOGY.

UPDATE: CIUDAD BLANCA HAS BEEN A SOURCE OF MYTH, ADVENTURE, AND SCIENCE FOR

CENTURIES. IT EVEN SHOWS ON MODERN MAPS AS A QUESTION MARK IN THE MOSQUITIA JUNGLE. SEVERAL EXPEDITIONS DURING THE LAST CENTURY HAVE EITHER FAILED TO RETURN OR HAVE FAILED TO FIND CONCLUSIVE EVIDENCE OF A "LOST CITY". MANY ARTIFACTS SUGGESTING THE PRESENCE OF A SOPHISTICATED CIVIILIZATION (OTHER THAN MAYA) HAVE BEEN FOUND IN THE JUNGLE SURROUNDING THE AREA WHERE THE WHITE CITY IS SUPPOSED TO BE.

ARCHEAOLOGISTS HAVE FOUND NUMEROUS SMALL CITIES IN THE OUTLYING AREAS OF THE MOSQUITIA JUNGLE. THEY HAVE SUGGESTED THAT THESE TOWNS ARE SATELLITES TO A MUCH LARGER, AS YET UNFOUND, CAPITOL CITY. THE DIFFICULTY OF THE TERRAIN, THE RELUCTANCE OF NATIVE PEOPLES TO VENTURE IN THIS AREA (DUE TO SUPERSTITIONS), AND THE POLITICAL STRIFE OF RECENT DECADES HAS KEPT EXPLORATION TO A MINIMUM...

... STEVE MORGAN HAS MADE NUMEROUS FORAYS TO THIS AREA OVER THE LAST 10 YEARS TRYING TO UNRAVEL THE MYSTERY OF THE WHITE CITY. TWO YEARS AGO HE HEARD OF A LEGENDARY GIANT REPTILE THAT GUARDED THE WAY TO CIUDAD BLANCA. THE LIZARD ALLEGEDLY LIVED FAR UP A RIVER IN THE HEART OF MOSQUITIA. STEVE PADDLED 5 DAYS UPRIVER AND FOUND THE LIZARD. IT WAS A GIANT ROCK CARVED INTO THE HEAD OF AN IGUANA! NEARBY WAS ANOTHER ROCK WITH STRANGE INCRIPTIONS CARVED IN IT.

HEAVY RAINS FORCED STEVE TO RETURN. INSPIRED BY HIS FINDING THE SOURCE OF A LEGEND, STEVE FELT HE WAS ON THE RIGHT TRACK. HE SPENT THE NEXT TWO YEARS INTERROGATING THE NATIVE PEOPLE ABOUT THIER LEGENDS AND KNOWLEDGE OF THE ALLEGED "WHITE CITY" AREA.

STUDYING THE INCRIPTIONS ON THE ROCK NEAR THE IGUANA CARVING, STEVE CONCLUDED THAT THE CARVING WAS IN ACTUALITY A MAP TO THE WHITE CITY. HE ASSUMED THAT THE IGUANA HEAD MARKED A TERRITORY AND THE "MAP' SHOWED RIVER TRAVELERS WHERE TO GO.

MORGAN CONFIRMED HIS THEORY BY OVERLAYING AERIAL PHOTOS AND TOPOGRAPHICAL MAPS ON A PHOTO OF THE "MAP" ROCK. AFTER MUCH STUDY IT BECAME CLEAR THAT THE INCRIPTIONS MATCHED TERRAIN FEATURES SHOWN ON THE MAPS AND PHOTOS.

WHILE IT CANNOT BE SAID WITH ABSOLUTE CERTAINTY THAT THE "MAP" ROCK POINTS THE WAY TO CIUDAD BLANCA... THE PROBABILITIES ARE QUITE HIGH.

ANOTHER BIT OF EVIDENCE TURNED UP LAST SPRING WITH THE DISCOVERY OF THE "CAVE OF THE GLOWING SKULLS". THIS CAVE, LOCATED ON THE PERIPHERY OF THE MOSQUITIA JUNGLE, HAD OVER 100 SKELETONS OF A CIVILIZATION UNKNOWN TO ARCHAEOLOGISTS. THE REMAINS OF A SIZABLE CITY WERE ALSO FOUND NEARBY. IS IT POSSIBLE THERE IS A LINK BETWEEN THE CAVE AND CIUDAD BLANCA?

JUST WHEN WE THINK THAT THERE ARE NO MORE MYSTERIES, NO MORE ADVENTURES, NO MORE EXPLORATIONS TO DO... GUESS WHAT? THE REAL THING IS ONLY A PLANE RIDE AWAY. IT SURE BEATS ANOTHER TALK SHOW!

- STEVE

Our 1996 Presentation

THE SEARCH FOR
SUKIA TARA
LOST CITY OF THE MONKEY GODS
A unique expedition and documentary adventure

Introduction

The expedition team is fully aware of its obligations to the people of Honduras. Every phase of the documentation, exploration and the scientific/archaeological results will be conducted with the participation and help of the Government of the Republic of Honduras. The site and all its contents will generate worldwide interest, but will remain the property of the Honduran government. The indigenous people of the region will be involved in all aspects of the process.

The names of certain contributors and sources have been changed to protect the integrity of the site and the security of the expedition. Full disclosure will be provided prior to the departure date to team members and financial partners only.

All material in this presentation is confidential. It is copyrighted and owned by Lost City Productions, LLC with permission granted solely to the Fund for Innovative TV. Any publication, duplication, or distribution in any manner without the express written consent of Lost City Productions, LLC, is strictly prohibited.

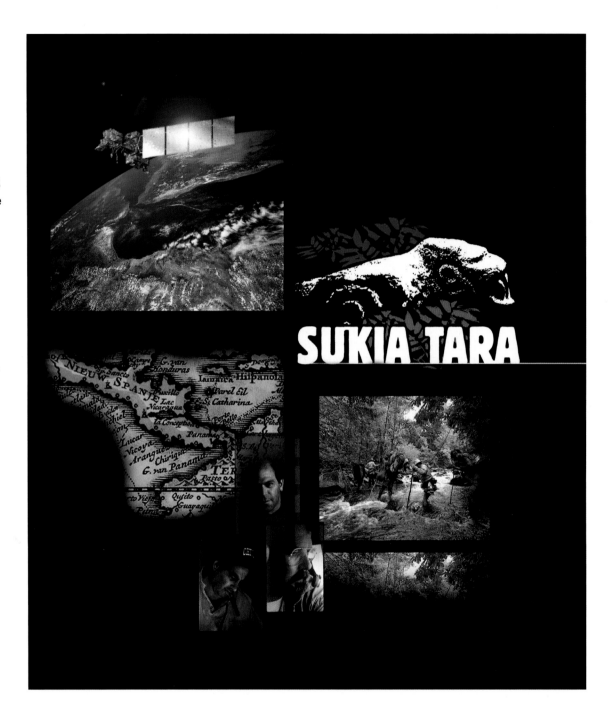

WORD IS OUT

"Scientists using images from satellites believe they have discovered a lost city... that could be the New World equivalent of Tutankhamen's tomb."
—*The Sunday Times*, London
19th October 1997

"Scientists are now scrutinizing enigmatic images...of a remote site in Central America which seems to show the faint outlines of a vast, unknown city buried in the forest."
—Douglas Preston in *The New Yorker*
20th & 27th October 1997

"...that space age technologies can be used to identify [yet to be discovered sites in Central America] is a marvelous advance for archaeology."
—Dr. William Fash, Bowditch Professor, Peabody Museum of Archaeology and Ethnology, Harvard University
Quoted in *Archaeology* Online Magazine
27th October 1997

Project Summary

In the spring of 1998, a close-knit team of professional explorers, scientists and film-makers will descend from the skies above Northeastern Honduras onto a spot deep in the heart of the world's most inhospitable jungle, where they believe the ruins of an ancient and as yet undiscovered city lie buried.

For some of the team, this will be the fourth attempt to overcome the hazards of this treacherous region. For others, as for the viewing audience around the world, the adventure will be their first.

Local mythology, accounts from previous expeditions, and the most sophisticated satellite technology have converged to produce compelling evidence of this city's existence. Now it's up to the **Sukia Tara** Project Team to prove the stories right.

"The geometric patterns that we've spotted are highly unlikely to be natural occurrences, and more likely, according to the scientific specialists on our team, to be man-made."
—Steve Elkins

Legends of the Lost City

Referred to in folklore as Ciudad Blanca, or "The White City," Sukia Tara has for many years evaded the best expeditionary attempts of man and remained the stuff of legend and rumor.

Evidence of the city's existence has been supported by strange artifacts brought out of the jungle by local natives, and by the tales of local elders and hunters most of whom, to this day, refuse to venture close to the targeted site.

In recent years, a few expeditions claim to have found evidence of the Lost City, but no hard proof or verifiable photographs have been produced to back up their stories. Several of these efforts have ended in disappointment or disaster for their participants.

In the 1950's, Jim Hanover (fictitious name, real person), a professional geologist in the service of a large corporation, was sent to the Honduran jungle to search for gold and ore deposits. Hearing the legends and the myths of this lost city, he decided to take time out from his work and confirm the rumors for himself.

What follows are brief excerpts from his personal logs.

Legends say that centuries ago, long before the Spanish conquistadors came to Middle America, Ciudad Blanca had been a magnificent city inhabited by a highly civilized people. Then came an unforeseen series of catastrophes. Some say that the people decided the gods were angry, and abandoned the splendid city. They left all their possessions behind them. They departed without destroying the city, leaving it as an offering to appease the angry gods. Thereafter, mortals were forbidden to enter. This was his account at the time:

"Twice I recruited small teams of natives to help me search, and twice I failed. [At times] the jungle foliage was so dense we could measure our daily progress in yards....

"A third time I signed on Hector Cavara, who said he remembered the ruins, seen as a boy 25 years before, during a hunt with his father. By the sixth day I was convinced that the reason the lost city remained lost was my [superstitious] crew wanted it that way. I swore the next day would be the last I'd squander.

"Late that afternoon I saw an unusual mound in the distance. It was like a giant ice cream cone overturned and covered with greenery.

"I unsheathed my machete and carved a path toward the cone. My blade struck sparks, I had hit limestone. I began to dig with my bare hands. In a few minutes I had my prize—the chiseled head of a creature whose species existed only in the imagination of its sculptor. At every step we found more artifacts... bowls, dishes, clay figurines. Darkness fell before we could reach the mound

"Next day we reached the mound at noon. It was about 50 feet high and overgrown with mangroves, ferns, flowers and leathery Monstrera leaves. I had hoped to find a temple, but inspection revealed only a couple of crumbling limestone walls and rubble. Was this the fabulous Ciudad Blanca? Or was this an isolated shrine?

"A view from higher up gave me an answer. Other mounds bulged out of the boundless jungle carpet flung out before me. I also discerned elusive ash-gray specks sprinkled though out the shimmering greenness. My nine power binoculars exposed them for what they were ruins of stone buildings.

"I found it...! I had found Ciudad Blanca!

"Using the mounds and ruins as check points. I outlined the rectangular shape of the city. I estimate that it covers approximately five square miles. If Ciudad Blanca was like other Indian cities of pre-Columbian Central America, then buried in the jungle were terraced temples, palaces, monasteries, observatories, colonnaded market places, ...I hurried down to begin exploring the city. Our progress depended on our machetes. After hours of hacking we still had not come upon any buildings, but we did spot a cornice sticking out of the ground.

"Attempts to dig it out failed because it was still attached to the top of a building! The passing centuries had allowed so much jungle litter and rubble to pile up over the area that we were actually standing on top of the city!"

"Jim Hanover" returned to the US and set up an archaeological expedition with an American university. This was to become one of several expeditions that were formed to explore these findings. All were to end in tragedy or disappointment...

At least, until now.

More than a Myth

After many years of traditional research and cross-referencing dozens of stories that have come out of the area, a diverse group of scientists, contemporary explorers and documentarians are now on the verge of what may be one of the most important historical and archaeological adventures of our time.

Team member, Dr. Ronald Blom, Lead Scientist at the Earth and Space Sciences Division of the Jet Propulsion Labs in Pasadena, analyzed infrared and radar image data of Northeastern Honduras from LandSat and JERS satellites, using specific GPS coordinates.

A co-discoverer of the lost city of Ubar (Arabian Peninsula) in 1992 and a leading authority in the analysis of satellite imaging data, Blom was able to distinguish faint indicators "shapes and lines that seemed to indicate the presence of man-made structures" in one specific area (an area subsequently confirmed as lying just a few miles from "the stone buildings" that "Jim Hanover" discovered). Closer inspection and computer analysis of the data suggested that something of unnatural scale and symmetry lay in the depths of the Mosquitia jungle.

Could this be the long sought after city of Sukia Tara?

The satellite imagery could not prove the city's existence on its own, but it did confirm a number of the team's suspicions and closely tallied with accounts of the city's probable whereabouts. Not iron-clad proof, but definitely compelling enough to create worldwide enthusiasm for a new expedition.

A Unique Media Event

Although the journey to Sukia Tara presents an enormous physical and logistical challenge, it also represents an unprecedented media opportunity.

As with other expeditions of this magnitude, the archaeological, anthropological and historical ramifications of a significant find are far-reaching and profound, possibly engaging the attention of universities, researchers and professionals for years into the future.

The **Sukia Tara Project**, however, has been structured to offer an additional level of involvement, namely the opportunity to observe a major expedition from its inception to its eventual outcome on international television, on the internet, and through daily news reports.

With so few terrestrial wonders remaining to be discovered, this may be one of the last opportunities to capture on film the very first sights, sounds and emotions that explorers have been experiencing for centuries.

Utilizing the very latest satellite, communications, computer and digital recording technologies, the **Suki Tara Project** will be brought into peoples' homes and lives with a reality and immediacy rarely captured: a truly vicarious adventure, with the same promises of discovery, danger, intrigue and surprise that the expedition team members themselves will be experiencing.

This is the **Sukia Tara** adventure.

•

Summary Of My 1997 Research Notes

Some said that the people in those jungle settlements were called Chorotecas—now extinct. Older than Mayans and Aztecs.

I read about ritual celebrating:

In one journal (not sure whose) the author reported that he had spoken to the elders of the tribe. Handed down the legends.

A version: "Small tribe made off with and captured 3 women. They took to the mountain caves, having sex with the men there. Children were hairy, half men, half apes."

It was to revenge the kidnapping as part of monkey rite to passage that they were required bring back three monkeys, armed only with 3 arrows.

They had to return with three or they were ridiculed.

Myth: The old toothless women chew corn and spit it out. Saliva and corn ferments. Becomes a drink.

Dama Sukya Tara (the head witch doctor) paints body with white chalk lines (stripes). Wears only loincloth. Has necklace of tiny monkey fetuses, teeth of forefathers, bags of snake venom and large crocodile teeth used as thimbles on fingers like crab claws.

Tribe makes a ring of bonfires.

Dama comes back with monkey on a spear and speaking in tongues no one understands, he places spear on the ground and grunts. Impales monkey then all the men bring a monkey and impale it into bonfire.

This is similar to what they do in Hindu rituals where muscles contract and sit up and make gestures. Guys imitate that and they drink the stuff. All the while, they cook it evenly on all sides—a la BBQ.

Then dama takes two yellow bamboo tubes in the eye and sucks monkey's brains.

He's the only one who's allowed to do it.

They eat and celebrate.

Lost City of the Monkey God—supposedly they found it uncovered part one wall clues given to them by many generations.

Info they got:

As you approach it, there are two huge stone balustrades with great stone carvings on one colossal image of a spider a huge crocodile on the other. This is similar to the Mayan ruins to the north. (Like in Copan where images of monkeys are also found.)

Several have written about the comparisons between Hindu monkey god Hanuman and this legend in Central America. Hanuman (or Hanuman JI) was known for strength and loyalty as told in Indian epic *Ramayana*. That's a different story than the Monkey King in the in the classic Chinese book, *Journey to the West*.

Lost City of Mosquitia has been called the cornerstone of an entire civilization whose population was spread out all over the region. These vast ruins got covered by jungle growth, but in their superstitious minds, nobody would go there. However, the old ones described it in great detail.

My Letter To Our Associates - July 28, 1998

Lost City Productions is now two years old as an entity. My interest and involvement in the lost city in the Mosquitia jungle has spanned more than four years. Some of us have been on this trail for most of this decade.

We have spent many thousands of hours trying to realize our goal of organizing an expedition and documenting it. It has always been–and still is–a terrific story. Compelling and magical.

We have exclusive scientific data and the involvement of some of the finest people in the field of satellite tracking of archaeological sites. We have done significant amounts of research and tracking of the legends, archaeology and natural habitat.

We have also spent a great deal of money and continually tried to gain permission and cooperation from the proper authorities in Honduras.

We have generated support and commitments from electronic media organizations, print media, and financial backers. All of that support is dependent upon our ability to legally and responsibly explore in Honduras. Without permission from the government, we are not likely to ever realize our goal.

It is almost September1998. We do not seem to be any closer to having that permission than·we were two years ago

So, as I see it, we have two basic alternatives–never or now:

1) forget about Ciudad Blanca, Sukia Tara, and the Lost City.

2) Exhaust every possibility for government cooperation.

Many in our families and professional lives would love to have us choose #1 and just forget about it. I don't want to do that right now.

I want to take our best shot. If that doesn't work in the next couple months, then I have to admit that it's not going to happen for us and we will throw in the towel.

What is our best shot? / I'm not sure. But I do know that I've never personally been to Tegucigalpa to meet with the proper officials. So, for me, that's what I want to do. And I need to do it in the company of fluent Spanish speaker(s) and someone who has familiarity with the people and bureaucracy of the Republic of Honduras. We need to be armed with a clear and simple plan which will be of direct benefit to the people of Honduras and one which we can definitely deliver on 100%.

The weather and other realities are such that we must schedule the first exploration and documentation for early in 1999–January or February. And then, assuming we are on target, to do the full exploration in April 1999.

The trip must be scheduled for October. So, who goes with me to Tegucigalpa? Frank? Marcia? Todd? Elki? Ken Lehman? Doug Preston? Andrew Jones? Clarence? Sally Station? An archaeologist? Begley? Someone else with connections there? We need to discuss this and determine the plan in the next few weeks.

That's my thoughts for today.

Letter of Support From Secretary Africo Madrid Hart - 27 September 2010

SECRETARIA DE ESTADO EN LOS DESPACHOS DE
GOBERNACION Y JUSTICIA

REPUBLICA DE HONDURAS   CENTROAMERICA

Tegucigalpa, M.D.C., 27 de Septiembre de 2010
Oficio No. 334-DSM-2010

Señores
Bruce y Mabel Hainicke
STEVE ELKINS PRODUCTIONS
Su Oficina

Atención: Bruce y Mabel Heinicke

Estimados Señores,

Sirva la presente para expresar nuestro interés, para que la Compañía Steve Elkins Productions, lleve a cabo el Proyecto denominado "Ciudad Blanca", en la ciudad de La Mosquitia Honduras.

Cabe mencionar que el financiamiento total de este Proyecto es por parte de la Compañía Steve Elkins Productions/Bruce y Mabel Hainicke, y que los permisos necesarios para la realización serán otorgados por parte del Instituto Hondureño de Antropologia e Historia.

Quedamos a sus órdenes en caso de presentarse cualquier inconveniente en el lapso del desarrollo del Proyecto.

Sin otro particular, me suscribo con las muestras de nuestra consideración y estima.

Atentamente,

CARLOS AFRICO MADRID HART
Secretario de Estado en los Despachos de
Gobernación y Justicia

My Briefing From Alicia Gonzalez

In 2011, Steve introduced me to Alicia Gonzalez, a Meso-American expert who had been curator at the Smithsonian Institution Museum of the American Indian. She knew her stuff and when we met at a deli in Studio City, CA, I told her I had taken two anthropology courses in college and was sure I knew almost nothing about the background of this part of the world and its history.

Over strudel, I asked her to provide me with an anthropology lesson on the roots and context of the Ciudad Blanca legend.

She was—and still is—super-generous with her knowledge. I did some book-reading and research, but this concise email from Alicia was the best way I could possibly learn about the academic background.

Re: Ciudad Blanca / Tom's Briefing

Tom, your questions are in Bold.
Answers are mine.

If the skulls in the cave were from 900-1200 BC, who knows what civilization they were from?

*They've now dated the skulls, bones and objects to an earlier date than what was originally thought. The dates can be extended from a time period of **1400 BC to about 800 -750 BC**. Although the cave was looted after 1994, and many bones and skulls moved or removed, what remained was studied in 1995-96 and this was what was determined:*

The calcite covered skulls and bones from the Cave of the Talgua River pre-date the Maya by about 400 years (the Maya dates are usually 1000 BC to 1521 AD). In fact, the bones and the objects within the Cave at Talgua River (Cueva Río Talgua) and two adjacent caves, the Cave of the Spiders (Cueva de las Arañas) and the Cave of White Stone (Cueva de Piedra Blanca), are considered to be from the Early Formative [2500-1000 BC] to the Middle Formative Period [1000-400 BC]. They are not specifically tied to any known civilization as such, and as yet they are unrelated to other Honduran non-Maya cultures.

The fact that these are ossuary caves puts them with similar caves that seem to be 'lineage burial caves' studied by several Maya scholars such as Doris Stone (1957). This means that small groupings of kin smaller than a village probably used the same burial caves. It seems that the Maya practiced having ossuary burial caves, as is the case in Copan and other important sites. Finding several 'ossuary caves' in close proximity and throughout a specific range in Honduras leads scholars to believe that cave ossuaries may be commonplace in parts of Honduras as yet unexplored. But the ossuary caves disappear by the Late Formative Period (400 BC -250 AD), pre-dating the Maya.

Of interest here is that these ossuary caves exemplify the small groupings of villages by kin and what leads to eventual chiefdoms or fiefdoms with a *'cacique' (ka-see-kay)* as the head of the *'cacicazgo' (ka-see-kaz-go)*, a local kin-based grouping, tribe, network of kinship or confederation with a chieftain as head. A confederation of these *caciques* is known as a *'señorio'*. Each of these confederations marked out specific territories important for commerce, warfare and other types of networking that included marriage, etc. (This is very important in understanding the nature of politics and leadership in Central America).

Social stratification is evident in the early ossuary cave of Cueva de las Arañas. The objects in Cueva de las Arañas or Spider Cave, yards adjacent to Talgua River Cave included wall art, ritual objects of pottery and riverine snail shells that were found in other Maya burial caves thought to be used for a ritual meal around burial caves. The offerings in the caves of ceramic and marble vessels were associated with particular individuals. Thus, individualized offerings are evidence of early social stratification associated with wealth and the development of social ranking.

George Hasemann was involved with the sequencing of a local complex closest to the Talgua River caves. The hope was to see if they were related and to compare the dates of the objects and bones in the ossuary caves with those of the archeological site that George Hasemann mapped. It seems that the complex site is of a much later period than the ossuary caves. The site dates to 600-900 AD of the Late Classic Period (300-950 AD) as compared to the 1400-800 BC of the caves.

If Ciudad Blanca is older than Mayans and Aztecs (which seems likely), again, who are the people, or at least what is some of the speculation?

Western Honduras is the farthest point of what is known as Mesoamerica, which extends approximately from Central México to Belize, Guatemala and El Salvador.

All of Honduras, Nicaragua, and Costa Rica are sometimes included in other maps. But what is shown here is defined as a region and culture area of the Americas within which a number of pre-Columbian societies flourished before the Spanish colonization of the Americas in the 16th and 17th centuries.

Map from the FAMSI site

Almost all of Northeast Honduras is not included, simply because there has been little to no research done in this treacherous region. Thus, to answer any questions about Ciudad Blanca, if it exists, one has to work one's way around it by identifying a vast territory which is sometimes considered an area akin to Amazonia in mystery, without knowing much about its inhabitants, its archeology, its history and culture(s).

So let's look at the known:

To answer you question, the northeast area of Honduras where Ciudad Blanca is said to be, is recognized as an area on the outside margin of the Maya region. It is known that central and northeast Honduras had a very large population, on periphery of the Maya cultures. It is also known that it is a region that has had contact with the Maya, particularly the formidable city of Copan in northwest Honduras. Scholars and others speculate that the people of the region *could have been middlemen in cultural traffic between lower Central America and the Maya world. Through them may have passed the gold-working tecÚologies of Panama and Costa Rica to the Maya and the jade crafts of the Maya to the rest of Central America.*

We can go back as early as the first Mesoamerican civilization, the Olmec who flourished from around 1500 BC to 400 BC, as compared to the Maya that begin about 1000 BC. The Olmec originate in what is now known as the state of Veracruz in México.

Marshall Saville, as you recall, has played a major role in identifying, researching and creating exemplary collections now held in esteemed places such as the Museum of the American Indian and the American Museum of Natural History in New York City and the Peabody. In 1900, he was the first to identify the 'Olmec style' with specific traits in a commentary on Kunz's discussion about an axe with a jaguar representation. Later, in 1929 Seville expanded his ideas about the Olmec as the foundational civilization of Mesoamerica. Research on the Olmec has been particularly significant within the last 20 years.

Most recently, Cambridge University Press (2010) published the proceedings of a session held to 're-think' the Olmec and to discuss new evidence of Olmec influence and style throughout a much broader area than had been previously recognized. Areas where previous research had already been conducted was reconsidered, and the review of old collections at the National Museum of the American Indian, the Peabody and other repositories allowed for a new reinterpretation that showed that the Olmec style and influence was clearly seen in Honduras.

Rosemary Joyce, an archeologist at UC Berkeley who specializes in Honduras, concluded that it was evident in artifacts found in Honduras contemporaneous to that of the Olmec that the

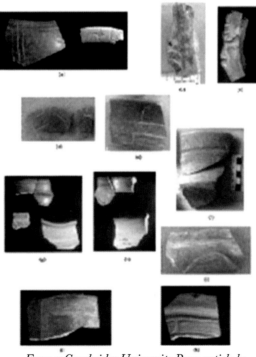

From a Cambridge University Press article by Rosemary Joyce.
These illustrate the particular features that are characterized as Honduran Olmec.

Honduran cultures of that time along the Ulúa River (and others) had been in contact with the Olmec to the north, and had adapted some of their artistic styles to their own, including pieces from the Talgua River Cave, and some from Puerto Escondido.

So what we are seeing here pre-dates the Maya, and in some cases are at the Early Formative at the very beginning of the Olmec Civilization. Obsidian quarries also played an important role, and several of these are found in northern Honduras, with samples of obsidian used for blades from quarries in Guatemala and elsewhere, evidence of early trade networks. Obsidian tools allowed for more elaborately made materials, body ornaments, etc. Thus Olmec style in Honduras illustrates that there were marked differences in stratification and hierarchy and that perhaps those who adapted Olmec features were of a wealthy class. The Olmec style also includes monumental stonework, which is evident throughout the known (and probably in the unknown) Honduran environs.

Language:

Now if we go on to another feature, language, and just take the Nahuat (na-wat) word, *Xucutaco* (shoe-coo-ta-coe) (Nahuatl) and the Mayan, *Hueitapalan* (way-tah-pa-lawn) Mayan, the names for Ciudad Blanca that Hernán Cortes used in his letter of 1526 to the King of Spain, we know that the ancient speakers of language early Maya and Aztecs used, had already been to the Ciudad Blanca.

On the border of Honduras with El Salvador we have the Pipil speakers, of the Uto-Aztecan language group that includes in the United States the language of the Hopi (Arizona), Ute-Pauite (Utah), and many others in California and Northern Mexico. The Pipil language is almost extinct. Then there is the Chorti, which is a Mayan language, found around Copan. (There are now only 10 speakers of this language and it is also almost extinct.

Honduras has other languages nearly extinct, such as the Lenca, although the Lenca people number 100,000. And there are also other languages that are quite revealing about ancient contact with peoples of a similar language. The Tol is a language isolate that I have been interested in for years. It is of the Hokan language family, one of the most ancient of North America. Its closest links are another isolate group in Oaxaca, and some of the peoples around the Grand Canyon.

Honduras has a mercantile language, the Miskito. This trade language is found in the Gracias A Dios Department, and it has 6 dialects in Honduras, with many speakers in Nicaragua. It is a thriving language.

Closer to Ciudad Blanca, and the name most often used with the Theodore Morde catalogue of objects is Sumo TawaŠa. There are about 700 speakers of the language, and about 800 to 1,000 from this etŮic group that live around the banks of the Río Patuca and the Gracias a Dios and parts of the Olancho Departments. But they are quickly becoming integrated with the Miskito. They are mostly hunter-gatherers, fishermen, and swidden agriculturalists. There are speakers of this language in Nicaragua as well.

It is the Pech whose name for the Ciudad Blanca is *Kaha Kamasa*. And it is said that they are the ones who believe Ciudad Blanca was built by lightning and thunder. The Pech number about 990 current speakers, while their etŮic population is about 2,586. They are in the north central coast, Municipio Dulce Nombre de Culmí, Olancho Department, Santa María del Carbón, and also in Las Marías, Gracias a Dios, Silín and Colón. The Pech belong to the Chibchan/Paya language family, found also in Colombia, Ecuador, Panama, Costa Rica and Nicaragua.

So there you have it. Ciudad Blanca is surrounded by all of these clues of ancient indigenous peoples who have been heavily engaged in trade that seem to go as far north as Utah and as far south as Ecuador. It has it's own indigenous trade language (Miskito). It is an early known source of gold and silver, with mines in the same Department. The use of monumental stonework and marble is very early, and

ties to the foundational civilizations of Mesoamerica are evident.

A Chronology of Ancient of Civilizations

Here for your perusal is a timeline to help you situate the chronology for the Mesoamerican civilizations and cultures. I did not include the Paleo-Indian and Archaic that precede the Formative.

Pre-Classic Period or Formative

1500 B.C.-A.D. 300
• Olmec 1200-400 B.C.
• Zapotec (Oaxaca, Mex)500 B.C.-A.D. 1000
• Maya (Mexico to Honduras) 1000 B.C.-A.D. 1521
• Teotihuacán (Central México)A.D. 1-650

Overlaps the:
• *Early Formative 2500-1000 B.C.*
• *Middle Formative 1000-400 B.C.*
• *Late Formative 400 B.C.-A.D. 250*

Classic Period
A.D.
300-950

• Zapotec (Oaxaca) 500 B.C.-A.D. 1000
• Maya 1000 B.C.-A.D. 1521
• Teotihuacán (Central México)A.D. 1-650
• El Tajin (Veracruz, Mex._A.D. 550-1100
• Mixtec (Oaxaca, Mex.) A.D. 900-1521

Post Classic Period
A.D.
950-1521

• El Tajin (Veracruz, Mex) A.D. 550-1100
• Mixtec (Oaxaca, Mex) A.D. 900-1521
• Aztec A.D. 1200-1521

Our PowerPoint Presentation - May 27, 2011

Ciudad Blanca - The Lost City of Honduras
The Legend of The Lost City

The Mission

Our team has been working to discover the Lost City for more than 16 years.

We have slogged through the dangerous jungle, commissioned revealing satellite photos, identified a target site, completed a fly-over, and taken aerial video and photographs. We have interviewed and collected data from explorers, archaeologists and other scientists who have first-hand knowledge and experience relating to the Lost City.

Steve Elkins was joined in his early jungle explorations in 1994-5 by international explorers, archaeologists and guides from the indigenous population. He has recorded important interviews with the late geologist Sam Glassmire who claimed to have visited the site in 1959, as well as Dr. George Hasemann, the former chief archaeologist of the Instituto Hondureno de Antropologia e Historia, an internationally recognized scholar who has studied the area for many years.

Tom Weinberg flew over the target site in 1998 and his documentation helped confirm what was revealed in satellite images interpreted by colleagues from the Jet Propulsion Laboratory.

Now, due to advances in terrestrial scanning tecÚologies, it is possible to effectively search areas previously considered impossible to explore.

The Team

Steve Elkins - Project Director
Tom Weinberg - Executive Producer
Dr. Alicia M. Gonzalez - Chief Researcher
Virgilio Parades Trapero – Director of the Instituto Hondureno de Antropologia e Historia (IHAH)
Dr. George Rossman - Science Advisor
Bruce Heinicke - Veteran Explorer
Marion Renk-Rosenthal - Journalist and Adventurer
Brian Musburger & Todd Musburger - Business & Legal Affairs

Steve Elkins
Project Director

Steve Elkins has a degree in Earth Science and has been an avid amateur archeologist for forty years. He is an Emmy award winning videographer who has collaborated on productions in hazardous and remote locations around the world including working with the late Steve Irwin (Crocodile Hunter) for many years. He was on the team that initially organized the archaeological exploration of "The Cave of the Glowing Skulls" at Talgua Cave in Honduras (carbon-dated to 800-1000 B.C.) in 1994. Elkins has also received a Gold Medal from the New York Film Festival, two Cine Golden Eagles, and a Telly for his camerawork and editing. Additionally he worked as cinematographer on two productions awarded Grand Jury Prizes at the Sundance Film Festival.

Steve has filmed in Honduras on four separate occasions including a jungle expedition he organized in 1994 which became the framework for a fictional mystery novel (The Codex) by famed author, Doug Preston. It was also the inspiration for Steve's interest in Ciudad Blanca.

In addition to "hands on" production experience, Elkins was also a partner in a broadcast equipment rental and production services company (BERC/Pal America) with offices in Burbank, San Diego, Atlanta, Hong Kong, and Paris. Besides renting a full range of production gear, the Company specialized in providing contract production services for domestic and foreign broadcasters working in many countries.

Steve's years of worldwide experience, most prominently his four separate film ventures occurring in the hazardous jungles of Honduras, coupled with his unparalleled attention to production details, clearly establish his credentials as leader of this project.

Tom Weinberg
Executive Producer

Mr. Weinberg is a nationally recognized television producer with four Emmy Awards and a Columbia University-duPont award for his non-fiction programming. He has produced more than 500 programs that have appeared on Public Television and commercial stations.

Mr. Weinberg was the creator and Executive Producer of "The 90's", a highly acclaimed innovative series of 52 one-hour non-fiction broadcasts on PBS in the early 90's. He founded and for 12 years produced Image Union, featuring the work of independent producers from around the world on WTTW/Chicago. His productions have appeared in the US on WGN-TV, MTV, WNET, Conus and FOX. Internationally his work has been broadcast on NHK and TBS in Japan, the BBC, Channel 4, CBC, Australian, Brazilian and Mexican TV. His work has been exhibited in the Museum of Broadcasting, the Pompidou Centre, the Museum of Modern Art, Whitney Museum, Rio Cine (Brazil) and featured in numerous festivals worldwide.

Mr. Weinberg has traveled to Central America more than two dozen times and has been actively involved in the search for the Lost City since 1994. His taste for Honduran cigars dates back to 1966.

In addition to his television/video career, Weinberg has also been involved in several successful entrepreneurial ventures including part ownership of the Chicago White Sox with Bill Veeck. Mr. Weinberg, 66, has a BA (University of Michigan) and an MBA (NYU). He lives in Chicago, and is the President of the Fund for Innovative TV which operates the streaming website *http://mediaburn.org*.

Dr. Alicia M. González
Chief Researcher

Dr. Gonzalez is an independent scholar, anthropologist-folklorist, writer and museum consultant. She received her Ph.D. in Anthropology from the University of Texas at Austin, where she was a Rockefeller Fellow.

Dr. Gonzalez worked for 20 years at the Smithsonian Institution in various capacities, including as a Director of the Smithsonian's Interdisciplinary Quincentenary Programs, overseeing programs and exhibits from 17 museums and offices.

She was Senior Curator at the National Museum of the American Indian, where her research and exhibits focused on Mesoamerican cultures and sacred sites. Some of her research, books, articles, exhibits and lectures include the following subjects: Trans-Atlantic and Trans-Pacific migration and trade, Mesoamerican trade routes and sacred sites, indigenous cultures of the Americas, the Manila Galleon trade, trade routes from the Mediterranean to Iberia and México, Pre-Columbian and Viceregal México, traditional and folk art of Japan, China and Latin America, Chinese influences on Latin American aesthetics.

She has worked as consulting scholar for several PBS series, including *Carlos Fuentes' The Buried Mirror: Reflections on Spain and the New World*.

Dr. George Rossman
Science Advisor

Dr. Rossman is currently the Eleanor and JoÚ R. McMillian Professor of Mineralogy at the California Institute of TecÚology. He has an impeccable reputation as a research scientist and teacher for nearly 40 years.

In addition, Dr. Rossman is recognized as a highly cited author in scientific journals with over 260 papers and has been the recipient of prestigious awards such as the Richard Feynman Prize, the Friedrich-Becke Medal, and the inaugural Dana Medal. His professional travels have taken him all over the world including the jungles of Brazil, Bolivia, and Myanmar.

Dr. Rossman is a popular speaker at professional symposiums and often works as consultant to major corporations and government agencies including NASA and The White House.

Marion Renk-Rosenthal
Journalist and Adventurer

Marion Renk-Rosenthal has worked with Steve Elkins since the first expedition to Honduras in 1994. Her role as a journalist and media producer were integral in the financial and media success of many of the projects they worked on together.

Marion hails from Hamburg, Germany and received a Bachelors degree in Macroeconomics from Portsmouth PolytecÚic (now University of Portsmouth) in England and a Masters in Applied Foreign Languages from the University of Nice in France. She is fluent in Spanish, German, English, and French.

Renk-Rosenthal has hosted radio and television shows as on-air talent for RTL and also worked as a broadcast and print journalist covering a wide range of topics across the world for European media companies. In additionMarion has authored two travel books. She holds dual citizenship (German and USA) and resides in California.

Todd & Brian Musburger
Legal & Business Affairs

Todd and Brian Musburger have a more than fifty years of combined experience in the entertainment industry. Representing pioneers in the fields of television, radio, sports and new media, they have negotiated nearly $500,000,000 in entertainment industry contracts with the world's leading media and entertainment brands.

In addition to representing some of the most acclaimed producers and directors in television, the Musburgers have negotiated record setting deals for television personalities, radio hosts, sportscasters and professional coaches.

Their clients have produced and directed thousands of hours of award winning programing broadcast around the world.

Bruce Heinicke
Veteran Explorer

Bruce has more than 30 years experience as a veteran explorer throughout the world. Originally hailing from St. Louis, he spent his early years combing through Civil War battle sites in the midwest and south. His keen interest in the ancient history of the Americas led him to pursue a lifetime of important expeditions both underwater and in the jungles of Honduras, Guatemala, Nicaragua, Columbia, Ecuador, Peru, Panama, Jamaica, and the Philippines.

Bruce is married to **Mabel** (a Hondurena) and lived in Honduras for many years. Their extensive knowledge of local culture as well as their numerous contacts makes them the team's leaders in handling the intricate discussions with local officials.

LIDAR

LIDAR tecÚology was first applied to archaeological investigation in 2010. Advanced Aerial LIDAR is a method of scanning an area from an aircraft with pulsed laser beams to create a 3-D image of surface features. Depending on how the scan is done and data processed, it is now possible to "see" through the jungle canopy and create images of archaeological interest (i.e.. ruins, structures, roads, waterways, etc. become plainly visible). This tecÚology has gained tremendous acceptance recently and has been successfully used for purposes similar to ours in other jungle locations.

We have selected the LIDAR group of the National Center for Airborne Laser Mapping because of their background and success in similar projects. Led by Dr. Ramesh Shrestra, this group is acknowledged as leaders in their field for their scientific acumen in applying LIDAR tecÚology for archaeological research.

Honduran Government

Over the past year, our team has forged key relationships with top Honduran officials, including President Porfirio Lobo Sosa. Eager to capitalize on this project's ability to help improve public perception of this troubled part of the world, President Lobo has committed to providing the full cooperation and support of the Honduran government with assistance from the Instituto Hondureño de Antropología e Historia (IHAH).

Most significantly, he has requested that Carlos Africo Madrid Hart, Secretario de Estado en los Despachos de Gobernacion y Justicia, personally ensure full cooperation from, and access to, all governmental and related agencies.

In the fall of 2010, the Government issued a Letter of Support assuring the President's protection and support of our project, granting us the exclusive authorization under Honduran law to conduct the necessary research and to explore remote areas as well as create, promote and license our findings in all media.

Lost City Productions, LLC.

Created for one purpose only, Lost City Productions, LLC., has enlisted a team of leading scientists and media professionals to locate the Lost City of Ciudad Blanca, using the most advanced tecÚologies available, and to produce and distribute compelling content surrounding this historic expedition.

Lost City Productions is currently raising capital to cover the costs of LIDAR mapping of the precise location of the Lost City, to be incorporated into a television production on the Legend of the Lost City and the many quests to reach it for more than 500 years.

The team at Lost City Productions will use its collective expertise to create strategic partnerships and divergent revenue streams so that benign exploitation can be maximized and to insure the historical site is preserved for future generations.

•

July 2012
E-Mail from Dr. Chris Fisher

I certainly don't doubt Begley's abilities or knowledge of the area—and presumably the material culture which is KEY. I also can't begrudge him not publishing given that he faces an uphill battle with his academic workload. But in the end no publications mean no advances, no students being trained to create the next generation of scholars, etc. He does know the area, however, the bugs, vegetation, etc. and that counts for a lot.

There is a fine line between being an academic archaeologist and being an adventurer—the public wants the latter (outside funding, Discovery Channel, etc.), and the academy demands the former (peer-reviewed funding, publications, tenure). In the end the two have very different requirements and moving between the two worlds is difficult. And probably a documentary needs elements of both. Despite my strong resemblance to Harrison Ford I've never really been able to get my adventuring career off the ground and so have focused on academics.

In terms of publishing a strong project design with rigorous data protocols that are worked out well in advance of any fieldwork would ensure that you can get the data you collect analyzed and disseminated quickly. I suspect that this is not that much different then organizing and filming a movie?

I also suspect that you have enough to publish a couple of papers already—could use the hillshades in ways that do not allow them to georeferenced. I can help with this if you desire.

Maybe the project could consider underwriting a monograph series focused on the forgotten corners of Latin America—it would be cheap and yield some street cred. You would be surprised how quickly some of your critics will change their tune once they can get a publication out of it—the currency of the Academic realm.

My Reflections on Our Project - July 28, 2013

We have made huge progress on the Lost City project.

To get to this point, it has taken 17 years, some $700,000, thousands of unpaid hours of work, piles of research and study in many tecÚical and academic fields, hundreds of hours of video documentation, tecÚological and governmental breakthroughs, unfailing perseverance, and a whole lot of luck.

But, here we are–just some $125,000 and four months away from actually checking out what we have discovered in the Mosquitia jungle in Honduras. We know the logistics and requirements for what we'll have to do...and we will go there in November and document it on film.

We know that we have made genuine scientific and historical discoveries.
The scientific and press reactions are irrefutable testimony to our success already.

We need to get to the finish line, which for us, must be to emerge with documentation on film/video of what we have done and the implications it has on the ancient and modern worlds.

We own all the media rights to the Honduras Lost City project. But, we haven't determined how to monetize it.

A few possibilities (after the November fly-over):

1) Sell the rights to our film/TV series to a media company. It could be for limited broadcast/cable rights. It could include product advertising or corporate sponsorship or global distribution of the film/ series we produce, or some combination that fits their needs and financial capability. We definitely need a financial partner in order to create the film/TV series.   OR...

2) We might find it to our advantage to do a far bigger partnership deal by developing an ongoing relationship with a major corporate player that involves our film/TV series, future productions as archaeological work continues, book, fictional movie, museum exhibits, marketing/merchandising (models, kids' toys, etc.) and many other possibilities. The partner would have responsibility for marketing, selling, distributing, etc. We would retain ownership interest and profit participation in everything that gets sold/ made/ distributed.

3) Turn over the entire scientific and academic future of the project to a foundation (such as CY-ARK, with whom we have been talking for many months). They would take responsibility for all the future scientific and academic expeditions. We would still maintain the media rights.

Much of the future has not been determined, but we do know a few things right now:

1) This is a significant historical and scientific breakthrough. It will have effects on future understanding of Latin American and world history and culture.

2) Our current need is to find a way to raise the funds to go to Honduras by November 2013, to actually see (and possibly land in) the discoveries we have made. One way or the other, we will accomplish this.

3) We will produce a documentary movie. We are starting now on the long process of organizing the mountains of video (and research) materials in preparation for editing them for distribution, hopefully in 2014.

4) It is an expensive project. Bill Benenson has invested the majority of the money into the project to date. One goal is to generate revenues to repay him for taking the risk. If and when it is possible, it's also a priority to pay Steve Elkins, Tom Weinberg, and others who have voluntarily invested time and money into the project for many years.

5) We want widespread and ongoing dissemination of the knowledge that comes from our work and the years of research that will follow. Included in this is the protection of the jungle, the site, and the entire ecological balance of the region. To this end, we will work with organizations and people who will best be able to accomplish these long-range goals.

My Documentary Vision

Lost City: The Inside Story (aka "Our Gang")
Memorandum for Bill Benenson and Steve Elkins, December 2014

We know the essential elements of our documentary:

1) the myth and history of Ciudad Blanca
2) the story of our involvement
3) the LiDAR breakthrough
4) the jungle discovery voyage and its ramifications

We must and can put flesh on all four of these. We already have excellent video documentation of the first three. We'll have lots more. Soon.

We have planned, discussed, thought about all this for years.

The main story is the "ground-truthing"—what we find and what we do in the jungle.

That's what will have the lasting impact on the audience.

But, it will take more than physical and social science to make the documentary itself as much of a breakthrough as the discovery.

My history and expertise is creating revealing videos--telling the human stories behind events. It's unabashedly honest, spontaneous, and rings true—showing how people react, live, relate, emote, and perceive.

So, I will create a series of **journal-like videos** that show and tell the informative back-story of the process that's happening in the main story we document in the jungle and in Catacamas.

Steve Elkins and his interactions will be a major focal point, but all our characters will be included—**Bill, Wendi (Weger, Bill's COO), Chris, Anna** (assistant archaeologist)**, Alicia, Dave Yoder, Mark Plotkin** (an etÚobiologist)**, the SAS guys (Woody, Spud and Stevie),** our video crew, **Michael Sartori, Juan Carlos, and Abhinav** (the LiDAR mapping experts)**, primatologist(s),** plus the **Hondurans—Africo Madrid, Vigilio, the IHAH anthropologist** and whoever else we encounter along the way, likely including some indigenous people and locals.

More than two dozen characters. Each one has a story to tell.

We will have hundreds of informal interaction moments to choose from…complementing the main story of documenting of the amazing voyage of discovery.

I have personal relationships with nearly all of them. I want to make use of the best small HD camera and wireless to tell stories that are totally unique…as interesting as the diverse people who are involved.

We never will lose track of the fact that this project is first and foremost a scientific exploration and adventure into the unknown.

But, it's also a human story.

And by finding a way to successfully blend our own stories with the science, tecÚology, and exploration, we will have elements for our documentary like none that I know of—a great film/TV show, that includes the people context in the process of making it, not a promotional or "making of" trailer, but an integral component of the overall footage to be edited into our doc, whether one film, a special or a series.

The goal is to capture the whole feeling of getting there and being there, following the threads as they unfold, from the U.S. to Tegoose to Catacamas and "Jaguar Valley," with insights from and about our truly brilliant and unusual characters.

It's a unique opportunity to simultaneously tell both the story and the story behind the story—and fold them into a revealing and informative final product.

We already have many hours of video that tell some of the inside story—from Roatan and from prior ventures. They will be useful. But, the mission/adventure in February will have a life of its own. The visuals and context will be stunning. It will have depth beyond the story line.

To communicate the sense of being there and who we are takes different skill sets than producing and shooting the mainline documentary story. **This is what I have been doing for 40 years in dozens of settings.**

I will be producing/directing this portion with one other dedicated skilled professional hand-held shooter of verité. As a team, we will be able to follow the threads I want to show. He will also have the experience and skills to capture lots of process moments on his own, using a wide variety of tools. (Plus, he can be a backup and/or utility, as needed for main shooting.)

Our film (or TV shows) will be **an amazing story of adventure and discovery**. We have a rare opportunity to layer it with video that communicates the uniqueness of the project and the people who are living it.

It will also have tremendous archival value for generations. You can only discover it for the first time once!

My goal is to refine the specifics of our producing in order to complement the advance visions of Steve and Bill and the team so it's ready to roll some **44 days from now,** our target date.

Draft 2.0 12/4/14

INSTITUTO HONDUREÑO
DE ANTROPOLOGÍA E HISTORIA

GOBIERNO DE LA
REPÚBLICA DE HONDURAS

Tegucigalpa, March 6 2015.

Jamie Shreeve
Executive Editor for Science
National Geographic Magazine
Washington, D.C.

Steve Elkins
Project Leader
UTL Prod., LLC
Santa Monica, California

On behalf of the country of Honduras and the IHAH, I would like to thank you for organizing and promoting the recent science and film expedition to the Mosquitia. Not only has the expedition brought global attention to the unique patrimony of our country but also provided a venue for positive cooperation between our government and yourselves to the benefit of all. It was especially heartening to have two of our own scientists be integral members of the team as well as provide an opportunity for members of our military to participate in a project they were very proud to be associated with.

Even though there have been some vocal detractors of the project for reasons we are unclear about, please know that the people of Honduras and the government stand behind what you have done. The UTL project followed all official protocols both legally and scientifically which has allowed it to become an icon for how future endeavors of this nature should be conducted.

Additionally, and perhaps even most importantly, your efforts have focused attention to the deforestation threat to both our natural and cultural resources which, without global support, is very difficult for us to control. We look forward to continuing our working relationship to sustainably conserve as well as study and promote the wonders of our "crown jewel", the Mosquitia.

Sincerely,

Msc. Virgilio Paredes Trapero
General Manager IHAH

Cc. File

Villa Roy, Barrio Buenos Aires,

My Twelve Steps To Exploring

Tracking Down a Centuries-old Legend

(as first told to 30 5th graders on June 3, 2015)

1 AWARENESS: Hearing about it. Reading about it.

2 INQUIRE: Ask people about it — lots of people.

3 RESEARCH: Spending YEARS trying to learn the REAL from the MYTH. from all sources: print, online, film and video.

4 COMMITMENT: Line up all the elements so you can succeed. You can't have a job (for example as a bus driver, doctor or lawyer) to do it right—discovery is a full-time job.

5 ELEMENTS: You need adequate MONEY—for the project and yourself. You must build a great TEAM—people who know the many parts of the puzzle you can't possibly know.

6 MEASURE: You must determine all the RISKS involved. Be cautious—it IS a jungle! And people have died trying to solve the mysteries. SAFETY is always the #1 concern. The responsibility is enormous.

7 TESTS: Do experiments to be sure you know what you're dealing with. In our case, a partial walk-in—1994; satellite imaging—1995; helicopter photo/flyover with GPS—1998.

8 TOOLS: Use best technology available. (LiDAR, 2012)

9 DOUBLE-CHECK: Be absolutely certain everything is together before you go—money, precautions, agreement with authorities (In our case, the Honduran government and people), and all necessary crew and staff geared for success.

10 GO THERE: Set up relationships and logistics *before* everyone arrives and do everything possible to avoid wasting time once the exploring begins.

11 PUBLICIZE: After the discovery, tell the world about it but always be honest. Don't exaggerate. Don't worry if others distort the truth. We experienced it so in our publicity and TV shows we never mislead. That's the only way to have control of public perceptions.

12 BE RESPONSIBLE: Do all that's possible to protect against looters and intruders. Then DIG responsibly for decades, setting up research and scientific/tourist facilities for benefit of Honduras and the world. The goal is the betterment of people everywhere.

Steve Elkins' email response to a draft of this book

Your comments about hype are good but you need to balance it with the fact that until we came along virtually nothing was known about the ancient Mosquitia culture. We opened the door to a whole new method of archeo-discovery and survey and created an awareness of the rampant deforestation that was going on which caused the government to shut it down.

The **Conservation International Rapid Area Assessment** (biological survey) evolved from our ground expedition in 2015. It was made possible by Bill's willingness to finance it, his long standing relationship as a supporter of CI, and my convincing the Hondurans it was worthwhile and to participate.

Without all the publicity none of this would have been possible—no further archeo work would happen, the forest would be taken over by narco-cattleman, and there would be no tourism infrastructure project happening in much of the country. The project became a rallying cry to improve the image of Honduras. Not too bad an outcome!

A lasting outcome as opposed to the work done by our detractors. To make things happen takes many skills and activities, and selling the ideas is always of top importance. Without the salespeople (in this case, the media), nobody works and nothing happens.

It is what makes the world go round.

INDEX

IMAGE CREDITS

Cover photo, pages 1-2, pages 13, page 20; page 31 bottom, page 40 bottom, page 46 top, page 47, page 84, page 88, page 91, page 93 left, page 94-95, page 99-101 top left & bottom left and right, page 102-104 top left and right, page 104 bottom right, page 105-111, page 113, page 115 top, page 116-118, page 120-121, page 123-126, page 130-143, page 146, page 152, page 153 right, page 155, page 164: courtesy **UTL/Benenson Productions.**

Page 3: **Grand Central Publishing, Hachette Book Group.**

Page 5 left, page 7 left, page 14, page 16; pages 26-31 top, pages 33-40 top, page 41-44, page 46 bottom, page 47-58, page 59 bottom, pages 61-70, pages 72-77, page 82, page 101 top right: by **Roberto Ysais**, courtesy **UTL/ Benenson Productions.**

Page 5 right, page 92: courtesy **Janet Elkins.**

Page 6, page 10, page 170: courtesy **Lost City Productions, LLC.**

Page 7 right: courtesy **Chicago Baseball Museum.**

Page 8 left: **Archaeology Magazine.**

Page 8 right: courtesy **Steve Elkins.**

Page 9, page 21 left: **Lost City Productions, LLC**, from **Japan Earth Resources Satellite 1.**

Page 11, page 83: *La Tribuna*, Honduras.

Page 12, page 15, page 19, page 23, page 104 bottom left, page 156: courtesy **Tom Weinberg.**

Page 21 right: **Insituto Hondureño de Antropologia e Historia.**

Page 25: hondurasculturepolitics.blogspot.com

Page 45, page 114, page 115 bottom, page 145, page 154, page 158: courtesy **Douglas Preston.**

Page 59 left: **Teledyne Optech.**

Page 71: **Virgil Finlay** via *The American Weekly*.

Page 79, page 81: **Commons.Wikimedia.org.**

Page 83: **Proceso Digital.**

Page 86-87: **NCALM**, Houston.

Page 89: courtesy *The New Yorker*/Condé Nast

Page 93 right: **Agence France Presse.**

Page 113: courtesy **Julie Tarbush.**

Page 128: **Picturist21 | Dreamstime.com.**

Page 144: courtesy **Christopher Dibble.**

Page 147: **www.na-pulpit.com.**

Page 150, page 157, page 163: **intervideohn. com.**

Page 151: Photos courtesy **mediaburn.org.**

Page 153 left: **Arrow Productions, Inc.**

Page 159-160: **Gobierno de Republica de Honduras.**

Page 161: courtesy **Elan Soltes.**

Page 173: **FAMSI.org**

Page 174: **Cambridge University Press.**